COMPREHENSIVE RESEARCH
AND STUDY GUIDE

BLOOM'S
MAJOR
DRAMATISTS

Sophocles

EDITED AND WITH AN
INTRODUCTION BY HAROLD BLOOM

CURRENTLY AVAILABLE

BLOOM'S
MAJOR DRAMATISTS

Aeschylus
Aristophanes
Bertolt Brecht
Anton Chekhov
Euripides
Henrik Ibsen
Eugène Ionesco
Ben Jonson
Christopher Marlowe
Arthur Miller
Molière
Eugene O'Neill
Luigi Pirandello
Shakespeare's Comedies
Shakespeare's Histories
Shakespeare's Romances
Shakespeare's Tragedies
George Bernard Shaw
Sam Shepard
Neil Simon
Tom Stoppard
Sophocles
Oscar Wilde
Thornton Wilder
Tennessee Williams
August Wilson

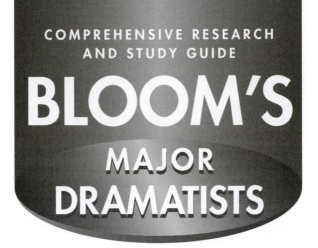

COMPREHENSIVE RESEARCH
AND STUDY GUIDE

BLOOM'S

MAJOR

DRAMATISTS

Sophocles

EDITED AND WITH AN INTRODUCTION
BY HAROLD BLOOM

CHELSEA HOUSE
PUBLISHERS

A Haights Cross Communications ◆ Company

Philadelphia SPS006 /526

First Printing
1 3 5 7 9 8 6 4 2

Library of Congress Cataloging-in-Publication Data
Sophocles / edited and with an introduction by Harold Bloom.
    p. cm. — (Bloom's major dramatists)
    Includes bibliographical references and index.
    ISBN 0-7910-6354-2
1. Sophocles—Criticism and interpretation. 2. Oedipus (Greek
mythology) in literature. 3. Antigone (Greek mythology) in literature.
4. Mythology, Greek, in literature. 5. Tragedy. I. Bloom, Harold.
II. Series.
PA4417 .S69 2002   882'.01—dc21
                                    2002151006

Chelsea House Publishers
1974 Sproul Road, Suite 400
Broomall, PA 19008-0914

www.chelseahouse.com

Contributing Editor: Janyce Marson

Produced by www.book*designing*.com

Cover design: Robert Gerson

Contents

User's Guide   7

Editor's Note   8

Introduction   9

Biography of Sophocles   12

Introduction to Tragedy   14

Plot Summary of *Oedipus Rex*   19

List of Characters in *Oedipus Rex*   26

Critical Views on *Oedipus Rex*

    Felix Budelmann on the Limits of Apollo's Responsibility   27

    H. D. F. Kitto on *Oedipus Rex* as a Familiar Greek Story   29

    Richard Lattimore on Plot Structure   31

    Herbert Musurillo on the Relevance of Plague Imagery   32

    Adrian Poole on Freud's Interpretation   34

    Rush Rehm on Freud's Interpretation   36

    Charles Segal on *Oedipus Rex* and the Modern Reader   38

    T. C. W. Stinton on the Audience in Ancient Greece   40

    Cedric H. Whitman on Oedipus' Ill-Fated Quest for the Truth   42

Plot Summary of *Oedipus at Colonus*   45

List of Characters in *Oedipus at Colonus*   51

Critical Views on *Oedipus at Colonus*

    P. E. Easterling on Three Dominant Images   52

    Lowell Edmunds on the Staging of Oedipus' Opening Speech   54

    Cynthia P. Gardiner on the Chorus of Elders   56

    G. O. Hutchinson on the Meaning of Oedipus' Journey   58

    Bernard Knox on the Historical Background   60

    Peter L. Rudnytsky on *OC* and Its Connection with the Oedipal Cycle   62

    Charles Segal on the Outcast and Reintegration into Society   64

    Roger Travis on the Authority of the Chorus   66

    Bernard Williams on Responsibility in *Oedipus at Colonus*   68

Plot Summary of *Antigone*   71

List of Characters in *Antigone*   78

Critical Views on *Antigone*

    A. T. Von S. Bradshaw on the Watchmen   79

    Michael Ewans on the Literary Origins of *Antigone*   81

Robert Goheen on Recurring Imagery 82
G. M. Kirkwood on the Contrast Between Antigone and Creon 84
Marsh McCall on the Two Burials in *Antigone* 86
Edouard Schuré on the Psychological Evolution of *Antigone* 88
David Seale on the Representation of Antigone's Opening Address 89
George Steiner on the Greek Notion of Invention 92
R. P. Winnington-Ingram on Human and Divine Agency 93

Works by Sophocles 96
Works About Sophocles 97
Acknowledgments 102
Index of Themes and Ideas 105

User's Guide

This volume is designed to present biographical, critical, and bibliographical information on the author's best-known or most important works. Following Harold Bloom's editor's note and introduction is a detailed biography of the author, discussing major life events and important literary accomplishments. A plot summary of each play follows, tracing significant themes, patterns, and motifs in the work.

A selection of critical extracts, derived from previously published material from leading critics, analyzes aspects of each play. The extracts consist of statements from the author, if available, early reviews of the work, and later evaluations up to the present. A bibliography of the author's writings (including a complete list of all works written, cowritten, edited, and translated), a list of additional books and articles on the author and his or her work, and an index of themes and ideas in the author's writings conclude the volume.

~

Harold Bloom is Sterling Professor of the Humanities at Yale University and Henry W. and Albert A. Berg Professor of English at the New York University Graduate School. He is the author of over 20 books, including *Shelley's Mythmaking* (1959), *The Visionary Company* (1961), *Blake's Apocalypse* (1963), *Yeats* (1970), *A Map of Misreading* (1975), *Kabbalah and Criticism* (1975), *Agon: Toward a Theory of Revisionism* (1982), *The American Religion* (1992), *The Western Canon* (1994), and *Omens of Millennium: The Gnosis of Angels, Dreams, and Resurrection* (1996). *The Anxiety of Influence* (1973) sets forth Professor Bloom's provocative theory of the literary relationships between the great writers and their predecessors. His most recent books include *Shakespeare: The Invention of the Human*, a 1998 National Book Award finalist, and *How to Read and Why*, which was published in 2000.

Professor Bloom earned his Ph.D. from Yale University in 1955 and has served on the Yale faculty since then. He is a 1985 MacArthur Foundation Award recipient, served as the Charles Eliot Norton Professor of Poetry at Harvard University in 1987–88, and has received honorary degrees from the universities of Rome and Bologna. In 1999, Professor Bloom received the prestigious American Academy of Arts and Letters Gold Medal for Criticism.

Currently, Harold Bloom is the editor of numerous Chelsea House volumes of literary criticism, including the series BLOOM'S NOTES, BLOOM'S MAJOR DRAMATISTS, BLOOM'S MAJOR NOVELISTS, BLOOM'S MAJOR LITERARY CHARACTERS, BLOOM'S MODERN CRITICAL VIEWS, BLOOM'S MODERN CRITICAL INTERPRETATIONS, and WOMEN WRITERS OF ENGLISH AND THEIR WORKS.

Editor's Note

My Introduction centers upon the *Electra* of Sophocles, so as to provide a complement to the Critical Views of the *Oedipus* trilogy in this volume.

As this little book contains twenty-seven interpretations of three major plays, I am compelled to be highly selective in this Editor's Note.

On *Oedipus Rex,* H. D. F. Kitto handles the familiarity of the given story, while Rush Rehm examines the Freudian strong misreading, and Cedric H. Whitman commends Oedipus for the heroic humanism of his tragic quest for the truth.

Bernard Knox gives us the vital historical context for *Oedipus at Colonus,* after which Peter L. Rudnytsky sets the play in the cycle, and Charles Segal traces the outcast's return to his society.

Antigone is illuminated by G. M. Kirkwood's contrast between the heroine and Creon, while George Steiner comments upon the Greek conception of invention.

Introduction

HAROLD BLOOM

Sophocles was a child of three or four when Aeschylus presented his first tragedy, in 499 B.C.E. At twenty-eight, Sophocles won the first prize competing against Aeschylus, and until 456, when Aeschylus died, there must have been many contests between the two. Sophocles's *Electra* has a complex relation to Aeschylus' *Libation-Bearers,* which was the second play of the trilogy; in Sophocles' case, *Electra* stood alone.

I intend to contrast *Electra* and the *Libation-Bearers,* employing Richmond Lattimore's version of the Aeschylus, and the new translation of the Sophocles by the Canadian poet Anne Carson. Carson, a major poet and a classical scholar, cites Virginia Woolf's essay, "On Not Knowing Greek," from *The Common Reader.* Woolf remarks that Electra's cries "give angle and outline to the play," and Carson (who shows a dark affinity for Electra) writes a remarkable foreword, emphasizing Electra's horror of the evil in her life, a horror virtually beyond measure: "she is someone off the scale." Strikingly comparing the Electra of Sophocles to Emily Dickinson's "equally private religion of pain," Carson observes that: "They touch a null point at the centre of the woman's soul."

Woolf, Dickinson, and Carson perhaps have only their literary greatness in common, and yet Carson's translation teaches us to uncover the Sophoclean Electra in the novelist and in both poets. Electra's grief is passionately personal in Sophocles, as John Jones noted in his *On Aristotle and Greek Tragedy.* "Personal" seems not strong enough, because we have debased the word, as when we speak of a "personal letter." That is too far from "Electra's private language of screams," as Carson phrases it, and too far also from Woolf's *Three Guineas,* Dickinson's Master poems, and Carson's tangos, *The Beauty of the Husband.*

In the *Libation-Bearers,* Electra is perhaps more angry than pained, a princess who fiercely resents her debasement, and who centers her love upon Orestes. The Electra of Sophocles has a death-absorbed imagination, as Carson says, and suffers the negation of her own sexuality. Here is Aeschylus' Electra, craving revenge, and unwilling to abandon life:

Almighty herald of the world above, the world
below: Hermes, lord of the dead, help me; announce
my prayers to the charmed spirits underground, who watch
over my father's house, that they may hear. Tell Earth
herself, who brings all things to birth, who gives them strength,
then gathers their big yield into herself at last.
I myself pour these lustral waters to the dead,
and speak, and call upon my father: Pity me;
pity your own Orestes. How shall we be lords
in our house? We have been sold, and go as wanderers
because our mother bought herself, for us, a man,
Aegisthus, he who helped her hand to cut you down.
Now I am what a slave is, and Orestes lives
outcast from his great properties, while they go proud
in the high style and luxury of what you worked
to win. By some good fortune let Orestes come
back home. Such is my prayer, my father. Hear me; hear.
And for myself, grant that I be more temperate
of heart than my mother; that I act with purer hand.

Such are my prayers for us; but for our enemies,
father, I pray that your avenger come, that they
who killed you shall be killed in turn, as they deserve.
Between my prayer for good and prayer for good I set
this prayer for evil; and I speak it against Them.
For us, bring blessings up into the world. Let Earth
and conquering Justice, and all gods beside, give aid.

Such are my prayers; and over them I pour these drink
offerings. Yours the strain now, yours to make them flower
with mourning song, and incantation for the dead.

This woman contrasts sharply to the Sophoclean Electra:

Alright then, you tell me one thing—
at what point does the evil level off in my life?
you say ignore the deed—is that right?
Who could approve this?
It defies human instinct!
Such ethics make no sense to me.
And how could I nestle myself in a life of ease

while my father lies out in the cold,
outside honor?

My cries are wings:
they pierce the cage.
For if a dead man is earth and nothing,
if a dead man is void and dead space lying,
if a dead man's murderers
do not give
blood for blood
to pay for this,
then shame does not exist.
Human reverence
is gone.

Electra is believed to have come late in Sophocles's career, and the celebrated irony of *Oedipus Tyrannus* seems far away. The dramatic ironies of *Electra* turn upon freedom, rather than knowledge. Orestes frees Electra from her immediate torments, but he has arrived too late to save her from the negativity that has become her nature. Knowledge cannot liberate Oedipus: to know the truth causes the agony in which he blinds himself. It may even be that pity in Sophocles is only another irony. Electra, in Carson's version, cannot be said to have suffered and then broken free. Throwing the corpse of Aegisthus to the dogs will not cut the knot of evils inside Electra. Her irony is simply that there is no correcting the past, least of all for women. ❊

Biography of
Sophocles

Sophocles was born around 496 B.C. at Colonus, the scene of Oedipus's death. Growing up during the Persian wars, he witnessed the Delian league grow into a despotic empire, ultimately falling into ruin during the Peloponnesian War. Sophocles lived in the most glorious century in Athenian history, taking full part as both a poet and citizen of Athens. The son of Sophillus, a wealthy manufacturer of armor, some ancient writers maintain that Sophocles was born to the highest station. In further support of this contention, scholars have cited several important relationships Sophocles had with leading and influential Athenians. There is a strong link between Sophocles and Ion of Chios (born ca. 480 B.C.), a versatile poet and prose writer to whom Aristophanes pays tribute in *Peace*. The two certainly met in Chios in 440 where Sophocles went as a general. Fragments of Ion's tragedies provide strong evidence of his being influenced by Sophocles. Ion also speaks of Sophocles' social poise. In Plutarch's account of Sophocles, we have further evidence of his aristocratic position in Athenian society, traveling in a "world" that welcomed such distinguished foreigners as Herodotus of Halicarnassus, a very distinguished classical historian. Indeed, Sophocles composed an ode honoring him.

He received a traditional education, studying music in addition to dancing and gymnastics, and won prizes for his various achievements. When the Greeks defeated Xerex in the battle of Salamis in 480 B.C., the young Sophocles led the chorus that celebrated the victory in song and dance, in part, perhaps, because of his personal beauty. Another one of his teachers was Archelaus, a Greek philosopher (fl. 5th century B.C.) thinker. Throughout his life, Sophocles was known for his handsome appearance, his grace, and his musical skill, as well as his genius as a dramatist. His life was for the most part a tranquil and successful one, with his dramatic career beginning in 468 when he won his first prize with the *Triptolemus*. In fact, Sophocles won no less than eighteen victories and never placed lower than third in a contest.

Sophocles held public positions of honor; he was elected a *strategus*, or general, twice and was appointed one of ten *probouloi*, or commissioners, who in 413 B.C. investigated the possibility of a revision of the constitution of Athens. It is said that when the god Asclepius came to cleanse Athens after a plague, Sophocles was chosen to welcome and house the god. In his work he was prolific and successful, and at twenty-seven, when he first competed for the prize in tragedy, he defeated the great Aeschylus. Thereafter, he was honored and rewarded for his plays and at his death was revered as a hero. In *The Frogs*, Aristophanes says of him, "[c]ontent in life, he is content in death." The great success and honor that Sophocles achieved suggest a fulfilled and happy man, but does not necessary support the stereotype of a life that was detached from the social problems of his times that some have come to believe he led. No writer has depicted human suffering and conflict with more understanding and truthfulness than Sophocles. It is helpful to remember Edmund Wilson's contradiction of the cliché. "Somewhere even in the fortunate Sophocles there had been a sick and raving Philoctetes." (*The Wound and the Bow*, Oxford University Press [1947]).

Sophocles was married twice and had two sons, Iophon, the child of his first wife Nicostrate, and Ariston, the child of his second wife, Theoris. Iophon became known as a tragic dramatist, and Ariston's son, Sophocles, wrote tragedies and produced those of his grandfather. There is an interesting though probably apocryphal story that Sophocles was brought to court by his son Iophon, who questioned his father's ability to conduct his affairs at the age of ninety. To demonstrate that his faculties were unimpaired, Sophocles read the choral ode on Colonus from the *Oedipus at Colonus*, which he had just written—and won his case as Plutarch reports in his *Moralia*. Shortly after writing this last play, Sophocles died in 406 B.C. and immediately afterwards he became idealized, in large part due to his personal charisma.

Of the 120 to 130 plays that Sophocles wrote only seven tragedies and a large fragment of a satyr play remain, although the titles of more than one hundred of his plays are known and some small fragments exist. ❀

Introduction to Tragedy

Origins of Tragedy

In the Poetics, Aristotle maintains that tragedy, the noblest form of Greek art, originated with the dithyramb, the choral ode sung in honor of the god Dionysus. One very well respected classical scholar, Gilbert Murray, contends that there is a basic relationship between tragedy and the early worship of Dionysus, with tragedy evolving from the *Sacer Ludus,* a ritual dance or sacred play in which Dionysus is represented as a vegetation deity or Year Daimon, the "cyclical death and rebirth of the Earth and the World." While some scholars have challenged this, it is generally held that tragedy grew out of the dithyrambic chorus which paid tribute the Dionysus every spring. From the dithyrambic chorus, Arion was the first to insert dialogue into the performance, which is to say he introduced the first real dramatic element. Thepsis, who is generally agreed to have been the father of ancient Greek tragedy, is believed to have introduced impersonation into the dialogue.

It is during the fifth century B.C. that Greek tragedy reached its peak with the three great Athenian tragedians, Aeschylus, Sophocles and Euripides. With the exception of Aeschylus' *Persians,* all of the surviving plays are based on traditional myths. Most of these stories date back to the remote past of the Mycenaean period, the great Bronze Age civilization which flourished in Greece from about 1600 to 1200 B.C.E. and, in all probability, these myths were handed down from generation to generation in an oral tradition. Thereafter, these tales continued to form the basis of epic and lyric poetry of the early Greek city-state, giving rise to such literary classics as Homer's *Odyssey* and *Iliad,* Hesiod's *Theogony* and *Works and Days,* and Pindar's *Victory Odes.* Tragedy begins with an oral culture of song, performance and oral recitation, as books were extremely rare. In addition to the epic and choral poetry which retells these myths, sculptors and painters illustrated these stories in temples, terracotta tablets, sarcophagi, bronzes, and an infinite number of vases. These tragedies, presented to its citizens on the occasion of great civic festivals provide an opportunity for the people to reflect on their place within the heroic tradition with the concomitant values and ideals which are the subject matter of myth.

While using well-known plots and characters, with which the audience would be familiar, each playwright imposed his own interpretation of how humans struggle to understand themselves, their fate and their place in both society and the universe. The general structure of the plays were: a *prologue* or brief introduction to the background of the play; a first episode, usually with dialogue; a *stasimon* or choral ode delivered by the chorus which is followed by a series of other episodes and choral odes, an occasional *commus* or lyric exchange between actors and chorus; and, finally, the *exodos* or last scene of the play, with the chorus leaving the stage.

The innovations that Sophocles made in tragedy were the introduction of a third speaking actor, a more extensive use of scenery than Aeschylus, an increase in the number of the chorus from twelve to fifteen, and the development of the single play rather than the trilogy or tetralogy. More impressive than these, however, is his imposition of his genius upon the traditional material of Greek myth. Sophocles' characters are at once individuals and universal figures, his themes deeply personal and broadly social. He is unsurpassed in his depiction of the suffering and dignity of man in his quest to learn the truth about himself. And that truth is both the terrible price and the reward of his struggle with fate.

Performance, Theater and Audience

The ancient Greek dramas were performed each year at Athens as part of the festival of Dionysus, god of wine, vegetation, religious ecstasy, the mask and the theater. Only two of the city's festivals featured dramatic performances, the Lenaea and the Great or City Dionysia, the more important of the two festivals. The City Dionysia belonged to the cult of Dionysus from the village of Eleutherae ("of the black goatskin") which believed that Dionysus had driven the daughters of Eleuther to madness. This festival, held during March and April when the city was filled with visitors, would begin with a procession bearing the image of Dionysus to the theater (located at the south slope of the Acropolis), and then proceed along an unknown route, carrying phalli, loaves and bowls, to the sacred precinct where animals were sacrificed and bloodless offerings were made. Both tragedians and comic poets competed at these festivals. The other Dionysiac festival was celebrated in Athens in January and February, and its name is a derived from the word "maenad," referring to the women who were driven to ritual frenzy by Dionysus. There was a procession and a mystic ritual and much of what is known is from the rituals depicted on the "Lenaea vases."

During these festivals, all the male citizens, and possibly their wives, along with foreign visitors, would assemble to watch twelve plays produced by three tragedians, each tragedian presenting three tragedies and a satyr play, which takes its name from the imaginary male inhabitants comparable to the "wild men" of European folklore. The satyrs had some animal features, were licentious, unrestrained in their desire for wine and sex. Interestingly, and in sharp contrast to the characterization in the drama, satyrs also conducted mystic initiation, and are depicted in funerary art throughout the ancient world. The satyr play took its themes from myth, with a set of typical motifs such as the captivity and eventual liberation of the satyrs, fantastic inventions, riddles, visitations to the underworld, care of divine or heroic infants, and athletics. Also in attendance at the plays were five judges waiting to award prizes. The performance itself took place in the open-air theater of Dionysus, constructed on the hillside in the area of the god on the Acropolis. The plays began at dawn and continued throughout the day with the crowd sitting on wooden benches, without intermission. There were no private theaters or theatrical companies, all performance being financed by the state and wealthy citizens of the city.

It is important to note that the plays had both religious and artistic dimension, beginning with a procession in honor of Dionysus, and included the pouring of libations to the gods, the display of tribute from Athens' citizens, a uniformed parade of young soldiers and a public announcement of the names of those who contributed to the city.

By modern standards, the staging was simple and the use of props minimal. All the roles were played by male actors, wearing stylized masks and elaborate costumes, with a maximum of three actors only per play, thus making it necessary for each actor to assume more than one part. For instance, the actor who plays Creon in the first half of *Oedipus Rex* later returns in the role of the Corinthian messenger. The chorus is, perhaps, the most difficult aspect of ancient drama for modern audiences to understand. Every tragedy was composed in verse, displaying a lofty and poetical style, which figurative and metaphoric language enabled the chorus to pose the most difficult questions, while the prose style of the actual dialogues was quite simple by comparison. It is important to remember that the chorus is not necessarily presenting the playwright's view but, rather, as Aristotle explains, yet another dramatic character within the play. The chorus is a public art form taking up such issues as authority, justice and the worship of the gods, all within the social framework of myth. Myth connects issues of ethical and political life with more personal concerns such as domestic life, relationships between the sexes, and weighing civic responsibilities against private desires. What the chorus does exhibit is a communal background and understanding of the unfolding action and, further, since there is no completely private life in the ancient world, the city's fortunes are intimately and inextricably bound with that of each individual life.

The Significance of Oracles

Oracles were the responses given by a god or hero when consulted at a fixed oracular site, and were the most prestigious form of communication with the gods. Oracles were numerous and were attributed with a vast array of powers as, for instance, the healing oracles of Asclepius, where the message was communicated by a prophetic dream with the addressee sleeping at the temple during which a god would appear in a dream with instructions, or as in the case of the hero Trophonius where the client made a simulated descent to the Underworld. The majority of inquiries are from individuals, although some oracles were addressed by the state, as when there was a concern about altering a cult practice. And the vehicle or technique by which responses were given were likewise various. The most prestigious communication was inspired prophecy, pronounced by a priest or priestess, probably in a state of trance in the person of the god addressed, and this would have been the technique of the Delphic oracle (Oracle of Apollo) whose origins date back to the very end of the 9th century B.C. The Delphic oracle, which was consulted by the polis as well as by individuals, provided important guidance in the formation of the Greek political life, offering guidance on such issues as pollution, release from evils, laws and cult. The cult history of the Delphic oracle is a myth expressing the chothonian, dangerous and disorderly aspects of the cosmos, from both the divine and human sides, thus offering men wisdom and advice on how to cope with the human side of the cosmic order. ❀

Plot Summary of
Oedipus Rex

A tragedy produced around 427 B.C., after the great plague at Athens, which scholars believe suggested the plague at Thebes in *Oedipus Rex*. It was written during a time in which Athens became the most powerful city-state in the world and was the recognized leader of many cultural activities in the areas of philosophy, literature, sculpture and painting. We are told that this play, on its first performance, only won second prize. Given that Aeschylus had already composed a Theban trilogy, which included a play (now lost) entitled *Oedipus,* it can be assumed that the basic outline of the story was familiar to contemporary audiences, at least to the extent that they could predict that Oedipus would murder his father and then marry his mother, both actions done unwittingly on Oedipus' part. Furthermore, it is also probable that the audience knew these offenses would be discovered and then made public. However, there are differing views as to where Oedipus died. While the *Oedipus* of Euripides (now lost) had the hero blinded by the henchmen of Laius, the traditions concerning Antigone and Ismene are not firmly established. What is most striking about this play is its irony, with the progress of the narrative consisting of an analysis of the past. For the audience at once realizes the dire consequence of Oedipus' actions, while Oedipus himself has no prior knowledge. *Oedipus Rex* is an ever-unfolding mystery, with each subsequent episode introducing a clue through the intervention of another character, until the final secret is fully unraveled. Furthermore, there is yet another dimension to the irony of *Oedipus Rex* in that an unspeakable tragedy is imposed on the framework of a happy romance wherein the lost baby, thought to be dead, is miraculously saved and restored and, finally, united with his parents. The ultimate and tragic irony, however, resides in the fact that this play is not about the punishment of pride, for the hero's deeds were preordained before he was even conceived. Nevertheless, Oedipus' truly heroic attributes—his love of truth, his intellect, his physical strength and integrity, and his pride—are all employed in the service of working out the pattern of his fate and the understanding of what that fate has been.

The mythic background of *Oedipus Rex* centers around the abduction of Chrysippus, a son of Pelops, by Laius, king of Thebes and the father of Oedipus. The oracle of Delphi informed him that his punishment for this crime would be to be killed by his own son. It is important to understand the significance of oracles, a form of divination, in classical Greece. In an attempt to avoid this fate, Laius pierced the feet of his three-day-old son and had him exposed on Mount Cithaeron. The shepherd who was ordered to leave the child to die pitied him and gave him to a shepherd from Corinth. Oedipus which means "swollen foot" was then taken to King Polybus of Corinth, who raised him as his own son. As a young man Oedipus was told by the oracle of Delphi that he would kill his father and marry his mother. Like his real father, Laius, Oedipus attempted to avoid this fate and left Corinth. On his way to Thebes he encountered his father, whom he did not recognize, and killed him in a quarrel. He arrived at Thebes at a time when the city was being threatened by the Sphinx, a monstrous creature with the head and breasts of a woman and the body of a winged lion, who had come to live on a rock near the city. She challenged every passer-by with the riddle "what walks on four legs in the morning, on two at noon, and on three in the evening?" Those who could not solve the riddle were thrown from the rock to their death. Oedipus was wise enough to know that the answer was "man" in the three stages of his life: the infant, the fully-grown man, and the old man leaning on a staff. Defeated, the Sphinx committed suicide by throwing herself from the rock, and Oedipus was hailed as a hero by the Thebans, who accepted him as their king. He married Laius' widow Jocasta, who, unknown to Oedipus, was his own mother; she bore him two sons, Polynices and Eteocles, and two daughters, Antigone and Ismene.

The **opening scene** is in Thebes, before the palace of Oedipus. To the right of the stage, near an altar, stands the Priest with a crowd of children, as Oedipus enters the stage from the central door. As the play begins, Oedipus, king of Thebes, addresses a group of suppliants, headed by a Priest of Zeus, who have come to ask for his assistance in conquering a plague that is destroying Thebes. Oedipus' concern for his people is manifested from the very start. He tells the suppliants that he has come to see for himself the grievous condition of the city. "The town is heavy with a mingled burden / of sounds and smells . . . I do not think it fit that I should hear / of this from messengers but came myself." Indeed, the very existence of Thebes is in danger as we hear from the Priest. Because of the plague the land, the herds, and the women of Thebes have become barren: "A blight is on the fruitful plants of the earth . . . a blight is on our women that no children / are born to them." Oedipus replies with compassion, expressing his grief not only for himself and for the suppliants before him, but for the state as a whole. It is also clear from the very start that Oedipus is held in the highest regard by his people, who worship his godly nature. "Noblest of men, go, and raise up our city." He explains to the crowd that he has sent his kinsman, Creon, to consult the oracle of Apollo at Delphi, "that he may learn there by what act or word / I could save this city."

When Creon returns he informs Oedipus that the city of Thebes is polluted by the presence of the murderer of Laius, the former king and that Apollo has ordered Thebes "to drive out a pollution from our land, pollution grown ingrained" and to find and punish the murderer of Laius. Indeed, the rite of purification is to be accomplished through the banishment of this criminal, "since it is murder guilt / which holds our city in this destroying storm." When Oedipus asks Creon what prevented the Thebans from searching thoroughly for the killer of Laius at the time of his murder many years ago, Creon tells him that the Sphinx was causing them so much trouble with the riddle she presented that they could not deal with the mystery of Laius' death. "The riddling Sphinx induced us to neglect / mysterious crimes and rather seek solution / of troubles at our feet." Oedipus' response is that he will once more make hidden things known, confidently assuming that he will solve this present problem. "Whoever / he was that killed the king may readily / wish to dispatch me with his murderous hand; / so helping the dead king I help myself." Yet, in sharp contrast, the Chorus of Theban Elders sings of its great fear and foreboding. "What is the sweet spoken word of God from the shrine of Pytho . . . I am stretched on the rack of doubt, and terror and trembling / hold / my heart, O Delian Healer, and I worship full of fears." The old men pray to the gods for help to which Oedipus responds that anyone who knows anything about the murderer must reveal it at once. If the killer admits his crime, he will not be harmed, but will merely be banished. "[Y]es, though he fears himself to take the blame / on his own head; for bitter punishment / he shall have none, but leave this land unharmed." But, if that person knows of, or in fact is, the murderer of Laius, he shall be cursed. "I command all to drive him from their homes, / since he is our pollution, as the oracle / of Pytho's God proclaimed him now to me."

The Chorus then advises Oedipus to seek the advice of Tiresias, the blind prophet. "I know that what the Lord Tiresias / sees, is most often what the Lord Apollo / sees." And so Oedipus sends for Tiresias, who now enters, led by a boy, and Oedipus beseeches him to answer in his infinite wisdom. "Do not begrudge us oracles from birds, / or any other way of prophecy / within your skill; save yourself and the city, / save me." But the all-knowing prophet attempts to avoid the question of who the murderer is, until a desperate and angry Oedipus accuses the him of withholding information in order to destroy Thebes. "For I would have you know / I think you are a complotter of the deed / and doer of the deed save in so far / as for the actual killing." Tiresias declares that Oedipus is himself the killer he seeks, "you are the land's pollution." But, despite Tiresias' difficult answer, Oedipus refuses to believe him and, instead, his self-doubt begins to feed upon itself, causing him to believe that Tiresias and Creon are plotting against his throne. "And now you would expel me, / because you think that you will find a place / by Creon's throne. I think you will be sorry." And, Oedipus' blinded insight is furthered emphasized when he chooses to construe Tiresias statement that he, Oedipus, is living in shame with his own kin, as a meaningless insult. "[Y]ou are blind in mind and ears / as well as in your eyes." Deriding the prophet, he reminds him that when Thebes was plagued by the riddle of the Sphinx, it was he, Oedipus, not the prophet, who solved her riddle. Tiresias continues to warn Oedipus, saying that this day will reveal his birth and bring about his destruction, but Oedipus regards these remarks as "riddles." And as he leaves, Tiresias comments ironically on Oedipus' great skill in comprehending riddles. "Shall there be / a place will not be harbour to your cries, / a corner of Cithaeron will not ring / in echo to your cries, soon, soon,—when you shall learn the secret of your marriage."

The Elders comment on the prophet's utterances, which make them fearful, yet they are loyal to Oedipus. "The augur has spread confusion, / terrible confusion . . . I never heard in the present / nor past of a quarrel between / the sons of Labdacus and Polybus, / that I might bring as proof / in attacking the popular fame / of Oedipus." When Creon next enters, Oedipus immediately accuses him of plotting against his throne and his life. Creon then defends himself reasonably, posing a rhetorical question to Oedipus: "How should despotic rule seem sweeter to me / than painless power and an assured authority? I am not so besotted yet that I / want other honours than those that come with profit." Oedipus' wrathful response is that he wants Creon killed. Hearing of his angry intention, Jocasta enters and tries to soothe her husband and her brother. When Creon leaves, Jocasta questions Oedipus about his anger. Oedipus answers Jocasta by declaring that Creon has used Tiresias as his spokesman to accuse Oedipus of killing Laius. Jocasta replies that mortals can know nothing about prophecies, that "human beings / have no part in the craft of prophecy." She then relates how her first husband, Laius, was told by a priest of Apollo that it was his fate to be killed by his own child. Attempting to prevent such a disaster, Laius tied his infant son's ankles together and ordered that he be "cast upon a pathless hillside," only to be killed later on by foreign highway robbers. Thus, she explains, it is folly to be concerned about prophets' words. "Give them no heed, I say; / what God discovers need of, easily / he shows to us himself." However, though her intention is to reassure Oedipus, her words only disturb him. "O dear Jocasta, / as I hear this from you, there comes upon me / a wandering of the soul—I could run mad." Her statement that Laius' death occurred at a place in Phocis where three roads meet, shortly before Oedipus' arrival at Thebes, makes Oedipus fear that he was indeed the slayer of Laius. Jocasta goes on to report that the one surviving member of Laius' party was a servant. On finding Oedipus ruling in place of Laius, this same servant asked to be allowed to work as a shepherd far from the city. Oedipus is now deeply disturbed. When Jocasta asks what troubles him, he explains that his father was Polybus, king of Corinth, and his mother was Merope. At a banquet a drunken man accused Oedipus of being a bastard and, disturbed by this taunt, Oedipus went to the oracle at Delphi to find out who his true parents were. But the oracle does not give him an honest answer. "But Phoebus sent me home again unhonoured / in what I came to learn, but he foretold other and desperate horrors to befall me, / that I was fated to lie with my mother." Hoping to avoid this terrible fate, Oedipus decided to leave Corinth forever. On his way to Thebes he encountered a stranger in a carriage at a place where three roads meet and, when the stranger and his companions attempted to thrust Oedipus from the path, Oedipus killed the stranger. He now fears it was Laius. There is yet, at this juncture, but one hope to which Oedipus can cling, the statement made by Jocasta that Laius was slain by many robbers. Oedipus asks her to send for the surviving servant in the hope that the man will repeat this version of the episode.

In yet another cruel instance of brief and illusory hope, a Messenger enters with the news Oedipus father is dead, apparently of the frailties of old age. Oedipus is elated with the news. "They prophesied / that I should kill my father! But he's dead, / and hidden deep in the earth, and I stand here / who never laid a hand on spear against him." But shortly thereafter, the Messenger explains that the child was found in the twisting thickets of Cithaeron's hills and, thus, the man Oedipus believed to be his father was in fact a childless stranger who had accepted the baby from the Messenger as "a gift." Moreover, as further clue to Oedipus' origins, the Messenger explains that the one who actually found and saved the life of the child was a shepherd. And in response to Oedipus' question about what was ailing him, the Messenger replies that "your ankles should be witnesses" to the fact that his feet had been pierced and fettered. To all of this distressing news, Jocasta continues to encourage Oedipus not to take this information seriously. "Why ask of whom he spoke? Don't give it heed . . . It will be wasted labour." Instead, she implores Oedipus not to seek any further about the truth of his birth.

Nevertheless, Oedipus is driven and compelled to find out the absolute truth, even to the extent of dismissing the Chorus' anxiety. "Why has the queen gone, Oedipus, in wild / grief rushing from us? I am afraid that trouble / will break out of this silence." When the shepherd finally arrives, a very desperate Oedipus threatens the old man with death if he does not fully answer his questions he so dreads to hear. The old shepherd tells Oedipus that his mother, Jocasta, gave the child to the shepherd through her own fear of evil oracles which foretold that the child would one day kill his parents. Oedipus is now fully overcome with despair and resignation of his tragic fate. "Horror of darkness enfolding, resistless unspeakable visitant / . . . madness and stabbing pain and memory / of evil deeds I have done!" And, while it seems that things cannot get worse, Oedipus learns that Jocasta is dead, by her own hand. He now asks Creon to banish him, "[d]rive me from here with all speed you can / to where I may not hear a human voice," while at the same time asking Creon to give Jocasta a proper burial.

In the **final scene**, Oedipus' two daughters, Antigone and Ismene, appear at Creon's request, and Oedipus weeps at the fate his children will be made to endure. "I weep when I think of the bitterness / there will be in your lives, how you must live / before the world." And, as Creon escorts Oedipus off the stage, the Chorus offers a eulogy for the ill-fated hero. "You that live in my ancestral Thebes, behold this Oedipus,—/ him who knew the famous riddles and was a man most masterful; . . . Count no mortal happy till / he has passed the final limit of his life secure from pain." As Bernard Knox (*Oedipus at Thebes*) has put it, the characterization of Oedipus, in its political dimension, is an amalgamation of Athens at the height of its power and influence and its confidence in human reason. ❁

List of Characters in
Oedipus Rex

Oedipus, King of Thebes, is the protagonist of *Oedipus Rex* and *Oedipus at Colonus.* He becomes King before his tragic past is revealed: that he murdered his father and married his mother, Jocasta. He stubbornly refuses to believe the truth until he confronts the old shepherd who saved him as a baby. Then realizing the horrible truth, he blinds himself in anguish.

Jocasta, Oedipus' wife and mother, and Creon's sister, calmly tries to persuade Oedipus that Tiresias' prophecies are false and he should go no further in his quest for the truth. She figures out the truth before Oedipus and tries to protect him from the discovery. When Oedipus finally realizes his fate, Jocasta commits suicide.

Creon is Oedipus' brother-in-law who has no desire to become King of Thebes early on in the play. This changes when Oedipus' terrible fate is revealed and Creon becomes eager to assume the throne in his place.

Tiresias is the blind prophet who reveals to Oedipus the prophecies of his past, and warns Oedipus that he may be the murderer of his father.

Antigone, daughter of Oedipus and Jocasta, appears briefly in the play to say goodbye to her father after Creon banishes him.

Ismene, daughter of Oedipus and Jocasta, also appears briefly to say goodbye to her father.

A **Chorus of Old Men of Thebes** reacts to events happening onstage and provides the background mood. It provides a guide for how the audience it supposed to interpret, or how not to interpret the play.

A **Messenger** provides evidence of Oedipus' true origin. ✤

Critical Views on
Oedipus Rex

[Felix Budelmann is a Lecturer in Greek at the University of
Manchester. In the excerpt below from the chapter entitled,
"Gods: A Shared Future," Goheen discusses Apollo's limited
responsibility for Oedipus' suffering.]

⟨. . .⟩ As I mentioned earlier, one of the rare statements in which a
named god is said to influence the action of the play is the one
Oedipus makes in the *kommos* of *Oedipus Rex* (*OT* 1327–30): ⟨. . .⟩

> Chorus Doer of dreadful deeds, how did you bring yourself so to
> quench your sight? Which of the gods set you on?
> Oed. This (*tade*) was Apollo, Apollo, my friends, who accomplished
> these (*tade*) cruel, cruel sufferings of mine.

'None of *this* (*tauta*) that (is) not Zeus', the Chorus (or Hyllus) say in
Trachiniae. Similarly, Oedipus holds Apollo responsible for '*this*'
(*tade*), which he then specifies as ⟨. . .⟩ (again *tade*) ⟨. . .⟩ ('*these* sufferings of mine'). What, then, is ⟨*tade*⟩? Not least since the line opens
a new stanza, spectators may make it refer to anything in the play,
including Oedipus' parricide, his incest and the chain of oracles and
events leading up to the present moment. ⟨. . .⟩

So much for the question of what Oedipus is referring to. In con-
tinuation he says (1331–2): ⟨. . .⟩

> But nobody else dealt the blow with their own hand (*autocheir*),
> but I (*egō*), poor wretch.

Rather than expanding on Apollo's role in his sufferings, Oedipus
now speaks of himself, explicitly excluding all second-party involvement (*auto-*, *egō*). Moreover, and this is remarkable, he does not
name a god ever again in the remaining 200 lines of the play,
whether in accusation or otherwise. Even the old oracles have almost
disappeared. Oedipus curses the man who saved his life when he was
exposed as a baby (1349–55), invokes Kithairon, Polybus, Corinth,
his father's house, the place where three roads meet and his marriage

(1391–408), but does not look for divine explanation. As Pietro Pucci says, 'even if we assume that Oedipus' emphasis on the human initiator of his story does not efface its correlate divine agent, undoubtedly he puts the accent on the human side of his catastrophic life'. After Oedipus' strong exclamation, it seems, Apollo has withdrawn. As one aspect of his desperate situation, Oedipus bemoans the absence of gods: he is now 'abandoned by the gods' (1360). ⟨. . .⟩

One reason, I suggest, why there is so much disagreement over divine responsibility in *Oedipus Rex*, is the absence of Apollo's name from the end of the play. On the one hand there is much in the play that critics, and equally spectators who want to explain why Oedipus suffered what he suffered, may use for saying: 'because of Apollo'. But on the other hand nobody in the play, neither Oedipus himself nor anybody else, says so. The end of the play takes a different course and gives critics and spectators little material to confirm speculation about divine causation. Apollo is prominent throughout the play but not at the end. Earlier I cited John Peradotto's complaint about Apollo's 'unresponsive authority'. He, too, can be seen as reacting, among other things, to the lack of statements about Apollo's part in the action after Oedipus' 'This was Apollo', which itself, at least in the first place, is restricted to the blinding, and which is immediately qualified by emphasis on Oedipus' own action. If little is said about Apollo's responsibility in the play and if he is not even named near the end, it becomes difficult for critics and spectators to make him 'respond.' ⟨. . .⟩ Critics and spectators are first emphatically directed towards Apollo as a driving force of the play, but then do not get the confirmation they may desire.

Uncertainty over divine and human responsibility, including the sense of a divine authority that does not respond, cannot be discussed exhaustively in the context of the *kommos* that follows Oedipus' blinding. Yet even this limited kind of discussion suggests that Oedipus is not alone in his despair at being 'abandoned by the gods'. Many critics, and in their own way no doubt many spectators, find it difficult to get the information they are looking for. Much in the play gives spectators knowledge about Apollo and his oracles, but in the end they need to infer many of the things they might want to know about him.

—Felix Budelmann, *The Language of Sophocles: Communality, Communication and Involvement*. Cambridge and New York: Cambridge University Press (2000): pp. 171–75.

H. D. F. KITTO ON *OEDIPUS REX* AS A FAMILIAR GREEK STORY

[H. D. F. Kitto is the author of *Form and Meaning in Drama: A Study of Six Greek Plays and of* Hamlet (1956) and *The Greeks* (1951). In the excerpt below from the chapter entitled "Middle Tragedy: Sophocles," Kitto discusses the play in terms of a familiar Greek story.]

The story of the *Tyrannus* is of a common Greek type; something unpleasant is predicted, the persons concerned try to avert it and think themselves safe, but in some natural though surprising fashion the prediction is fulfilled. Next to the *Tyrannus* itself, the most elaborate example is the story of Astyages and the infant Cyrus in Herodotus. What does Sophocles make of this ancient motif?

At the beginning of the play Oedipus is the great King who has saved Thebes in the past and is their only hope now; no one can compare with Oedipus in reading dark secrets. At the end, he is the polluted outcast, himself the cause of the city's distress, through crimes predicted by Apollo before he was born. Is this grim determinism? Is Sophocles telling us that Man is only the plaything of Fate? Or does he mean, as Bowra suggested, no more than that the gods have contrived this awful fate for Oedipus in order to display their power to man and to teach him a salutary lesson? Or is Sophocles simply making exciting drama, leaving the philosophical implications unexplored? There is only one way of finding out. Whatever Sophocles meant, he put his meaning into the play, and to get it out again we must contemplate the play—all of it, in all its aspects; not bits of it, and some of its aspects.

As in the *Electra*, the action shows a certain duality. In the foreground are autonomous human actors, drawn vividly, and complete. Oedipus himself, Teiresias, Creon, Iocasta, and the two shepherds, are all as lifelike as characters in a play can be; and so, in their degree, are the remoter characters who do not appear—the hot-tempered Laius at the cross-road, and the unknown Corinthian who insulted Oedipus when he was half-drunk. The circumstances, too, are natural, even inevitable, granted these characters. Oedipus, as we see him time after time, is intelligent, determined, self-reliant, but hot-tempered and too sure of himself; and an apparently malignant chain of circumstances combines now with the strong, now with the weak side of his character to produce the catastrophe. A man of poor spirit would have swallowed the insult and remained safe in Corinth, but Oedipus was resolute; not content with Polybus' assurance he went to Delphi and asked the god about it, and when the god, not answering his question, repeated the warning given originally to Laius, Oedipus, being a man of determination, never went back to Corinth. It was a coincidence, but not an unnatural one, that Laius was on his way from Thebes to Delphi. They met at the cross-road, and as father and son were of similar temper the disaster occurred. Even so, he could have arrived at Thebes safely, had he not been a man of high intelligence; for then he could not have read the riddle of the Sphinx. But again, though intelligent, he was blind enough to marry a woman old enough to be his mother, certain that his mother was in Corinth. The story is not moralized. Sophocles could have put Oedipus in the wrong at the cross-road; he could have suggested that blind ambition made him accept the crown and Queen of Thebes. He does neither of these things; Oedipus is not being given his deserts by an offended Heaven. What happens is the natural result of the weaknesses and the virtues of his character, in combination with other people's. It is a tragic chapter from life, complete in itself, except for the original oracle and its repetition. Sophocles is not trying to make us feel that an inexorable destiny or a malignant god is guiding the events.

—H. D. F Kitto, *Greek Tragedy: A Literary Study*. London: Methuen & Co., Ltd., 3d ed. (1961): pp. 138–39.

[Richard Lattimore is the translator and editor of numerous ancient Greek works, including Aeschylus' *The Oresteia: Agamemnon, The Libation Bearers, The Eumenides* (1953) and *The Odes of Pindar* (1959). In the excerpt below from his chapter entitled "Sophocles II," Lattimore discusses the general structure of *Oedipus Tyrannus* in terms of type of plot in which the lost one is found.]

The plot of *Oedipus,* beginning with the prologue and continuing through the next to the last episode, or act, concerns itself with the investigation of events which have already happened. It consists essentially in the joining together of pieces of information (*symbola* or "clues") until the last piece has been put in, the pattern completed, the puzzle solved. There are two principal problems: the detection of the murderer of Laius and the discovery of the identity of Oedipus himself; a manhunt combined with what might be called a rescue party. But both searches turn out to be after the same game, and the solution—discovery—is complete when the two are identified.

Thus, the drama belongs to the general story pattern of the lost one found. The lost one may be a lost husband, wife, brother, sister, or any close *philos,* thought dead far away but discovered to be present, unknown. A particularly popular variant has been the one that makes the lost one the lost baby or the foundling: the type to which *Oedipus* belongs. Whichever variant happens to be followed, the pattern of itself seems to generate certain features that are required, or almost required. For the foundling story, we may note the following: the child is noble; the child is unwanted and is put away (usually for destruction) and thought dead; but the method is always indirect (in Greek versions, a servant is usually delegated to do the dirty work) and the child is rescued, sometimes miraculously nursed by animals. The child grows up in the wilds, and is thought to be plebeian, but is at last recognized by infallible tests or unmistakable tokens and restored to its proper station. Thus the story is in part a story of the triumph of truth over rumor or opinion, and the triumph is pretty likely to come after the darkest moment, when error is on the point of prevailing.

A brief consideration of *Oedipus* will show that it follows the pattern almost perfectly. The tokens are not used by Sophocles toward the solution—he has another use for them—but they are there in the form of those otherwise so superfluously cruel pins stuck through the baby's ankles. It is also true that Oedipus is believed to be noble, though of the wrong noble stock: instead of being raised as the peasant's son, he is adopted by the great. ⟨. . .⟩ From the stories of Iamus, the young Cyrus, and Romulus, to the stories of Ernest and Ralph Rackstraw, the foundling story is a success story, a theme for what we call comedy or romantic comedy. But *Oedipus* is a true tragedy.

The tragically fulfilled story, mounted on so articulate a scheme for comedy, accounts for much of the essential nature of *Oedipus*. No extant tragedy so bristles with tragic irony. It opposes Oedipus— possessed of rumor, opinion, or, that is, error—against those who know—Tiresias, the Theban Shepherd—the latter two pulling back against revelation, because they know it is bad, as insistently as Oedipus, armed with his native wit (*gnōmē*) goes plunging forward. Where characters themselves are not omniscient, the audience is. They know the gist of the story and can be surprised only in the means by which the necessary ends are achieved. ⟨. . .⟩ Oedipus keeps circling back on the truth and brushing against it, as if he subconsciously knew where it was; the omniscient audience can only wonder when the shock of contact will come.

—Richard Lattimore, *The Poetry of Greek Tragedy*. Baltimore: The Johns Hopkins Press (1958): pp. 82–84.

⊛

HERBERT MUSURILLO ON THE RELEVANCE OF PLAGUE IMAGERY

[Herbert Musurillo is the author of *The Light and the Darkness: Studies in the Dramatic Poetry of Sophocles* (1967) and the editor of *The Acts of the Pagan Martyrs: Acta Alexandrinorum* (1954). In the excerpt below from his article, "Sunken Imagery in Sophocles' *Oedipus*," Musurillo discusses the relevance of the plague as one of the predominant images in the play.]

Even though I risk the wrath of modern critics, I should like to suggest four important qualities which have been found in ancient as well as modern poetry in varying degrees. They are i) the prosodic element (rhythm, rhyme, assonance, etc.), ii) a peculiar compression of ideas (which avoids the complete exposition of ordinary prose), iii) a kind of image-logic based on analogy and association, and iv) a special choice of words (again in a way that avoids the suggestion of prose). ⟨. . .⟩

Now in the *Oedipus* Sophocles proceeds by laying down a series of fundamental images; then, in the course of the play, the most important of these (the predominant or leading images) are taken up and developed like musical themes and allowed to acquire deeper connotations as the play comes to a close. It is this developmental process, and particularly Sophocles' use of predominant images, which we wish to illustrate here.

In the first part of the play, up till the end of the *Parodos,* the chief image would appear to be that of the great plague; and in Sophocles' hands it is not only an image but also a symbol. Further, it should be recalled that for the Greeks as well as the Romans the word "plague" had no definite pathological denotation. ⟨. . .⟩ In any case, how far Sophocles in the Oedipus incorporated the actual symptoms of the great Athenian plague, or what was the real nature of the plague as described by Thucydides, need not concern us here. But it may perhaps be important to note that the Theban plague created by Sophocles is not only what we today would call an epidemic (affecting human beings); there is, as well, a blight on plants (*O. T.,* 25, 254), and an epizootic among the cattle (*O. T.,* 26). Further, the symptoms of the epidemic are complicated by the occurrence of what would seem to be puerperal fever (*O. T.,* 26, 173–4), affecting, therefore, merely the women in childbirth. Now whether or not we may find historical examples of such a coincidence, the additional details of the blight and the puerperal fever are, I think, significant for the symbolism. For it would appear that Sophocles has conceived of the divinely sent plague as a daemonic force attacking the very sources of life ⟨. . .⟩ for Oedipus' unwitting crime has, for the Greek mind at least, caused a profound disturbance in those laws which govern relationships between parents and offspring. For this he has incurred a ritual defilement, ⟨. . .⟩ and it was only fitting that the penalty inflicted on Thebes should somehow symbolize the nature of the crime.

It is a commonplace that the Greek notion of ⟨a ritual defilement⟩ is for modern Western minds an extremely difficult one. For it was, in a sense, a kind of moral guilt without implying the full knowledge and culpability which we demand with our Western, or perhaps more Roman, approach to moral problems. But perhaps the best analogy may be taken from medicine. ⟨A ritual defilement⟩ is incurred as though it were a disease, without full awareness being necessary; it is infectious and can defile a family and an entire city, and even perhaps be transmitted by heredity; and it may be cured by isolating the defiled individual from the community and having him undergo certain ritual purifications imposed by the god offended or by his legitimate ministers. It is only, of course, an analogy: but it was perhaps some such association of ideas which for Sophocles made the Athenian plague (with the various changes which Sophocles adopted) an extremely suggestive symbol for the opening movement of the *Oedipus*.

—Herbert Musurillo, "Sunken Imagery in Sophocles' *Oedipus*." *American Journal of Philology*, vol. LXXVIII (1957): pp. 37–40.

⟨Ⓟ⟩

ADRIAN POOLE ON FREUD'S INTERPRETATION

[Adrian Poole is the author of *Coriolanus* (1988) and *Henry James* (1991). In the excerpt below from the chapter entitled "Questions and Answers: Sophocles, Shakespeare," Poole discusses the relevance of Freud's interpretation of *Oedipus Tyrannus*.]

Sophocles' play conducts a protracted investigation into the diverse roles which human beings play and fail to play in the composition of their own existence. These beings, or 'characters', are necessarily distinct from their experience, even as that experience is part of them. They are not, they cannot be, single beings; they are double and divided. This play does not represent a man doing the most terrible things a man can do; it represents a man's gradual discovery that he has done them. There are (at least) two Oedipuses in the play: the one who did the most terrible things a man can do, and the one who pursues and convicts him. To use a Freudian metaphor, Sophocles' Oedipus is not only the patient but also the analyst. Freud fails to recognize himself in this image of Oedipus' other self, that of the zealous, passionate interpreter. To use a Sophoclean metaphor, Freud thought that he had found a *symbolon* in Oedipus, a matching tally or 'other half' for the image of the self which he was pursuing. So that in matching himself with Oedipus in this way, Freud took over the role which Oedipus himself fills in Sophocles' play, that of the man who asks all the questions.

For Freud, Hamlet was always closely associated with Oedipus. Again Freud finds a likeness solely in what the two fictional characters suffer from, the desires with which they are supposedly cursed. But Hamlet too has a side to him that Freud ignores. What Hamlet has in common with Oedipus and Freud is that he asks a lot of questions. Freud sees only half of each character, the half that could play the part of patient to his own analyst. And in extricating them from their own dramas and recasting them in his own, Freud seizes the role of analyst for himself, displacing the Oedipus and the Hamlet who make such courageous efforts to understand the story of their lives in the very act of its composition.

The most significant thing that Freud has to say about Sophocles' Oedipus is to do with the form and structure of the play rather than its hidden content: 'The action of the play consists in nothing other than the process of revelation, with cunning delays and ever mounting excitement—a process that can be likened to the work of a psychoanalysis—that Oedipus himself is the murderer of Laius.' 'The work of *a* psychoanalysis': that is, the specific confrontation and intercourse between analyst and patient. This suggests that a psychoanalysis is constructed like a tragedy, or at least like this tragedy, and that what a psychoanalysis and a tragedy have in common is something to do with their work of discovery. In each case we are moved by the products of revelation only in so far as we are moved by the process of revelation.

When we consider the importance of Oedipus for Freud, we should therefore recall not only the image of a man who acts out our (supposedly) deepest fantasies, but also the action of the play through which Oedipus must discover the truth. If there is a 'compulsion' in Sophocles' play, it is much less obviously the compulsion to act out infantile fantasies than the compulsion to know the truth.

Sophocles' Oedipus and Shakespeare's Hamlet are the two characters in tragic drama most actively engaged in analysis and interpretation. Their importance for Freud is more to do with a passion for knowledge than with an occult or repressed guilt. Or rather, it is with their exploration of the mysterious relations between knowledge and guilt, a mystery which Freud radically simplifies by attributing guilt solely to the object of interpretation.

Oedipus and Hamlet are on their own within their worlds. Watching their efforts to interpret and understand from within the flow of their own lives, we recognize a universal predicament. Both Oedipus and Hamlet possess great powers of mind, but the questions to which they address themselves involve their whole being. The riddles they attempt to solve, the guilts discovered and incurred in the process of trying to solve them, these are written in flesh and blood; their own and others'.

—Adrian Poole, Tragedy: Shakespeare and the Greek Example. Oxford: Basil Blackwell (1987): pp. 89–90.

✿

RUSH REHM ON FREUD'S INTERPRETATION

[Rush Rehm is the author of *Marriage to Death: The Conflation of Wedding and Funeral Rituals in Greek Tragedy* (1994). In the excerpt below from the article entitled "Sophocles' *Oedipus Tyrannus*," Rehm questions the validity of applying a Freudian interpretation to a theatrical production of the original play.]

Long considered the 'classic' Greek tragedy, Sophocles' *Oedipus Tyrannus* holds a special place in the history of Western theatre. In some respects the notoriety of the play helps it work on the contemporary stage, since most audiences know the outline of the story. Compare the lack of familiarity with Aeschylus' *Seven Against Thebes,* or Euripides' *Ion,* or Sophocles' own *Philoctetes.* However, exposure to the Oedipus myth has its drawbacks as well, for much of the modern fascination with the play derives from Freud's use of the story as the paradigm for his psychoanalytic theory of male infantile desire. There is no denying the importance of the Oedipal complex as a psychological and interpretive model, but it sheds little light on the play Sophocles wrote and, when applied to a production, leads the audience down a theatrical blind-alley.

So, too, does the application of psychological realism to the play, epitomized by questions like 'Why did Oedipus marry someone old enough to be his mother?' *Oedipus Tyrannus* is not a cautionary tale of crime and punishment, where the audience are meant to think that Oedipus and Jocasta should have known better. The issue held no dramatic interest for Sophocles since it never is hinted at in the text.

A more insidious form of theatrical reductionism arises from the mistaken belief that the characters in the play are simply puppets in the hands of the gods. Although Oedipus is born to doom, everything he does on-stage he freely chooses. Even while matching his life to the terrible fate inscribed for him, Oedipus continues to act autonomously, following the best information available. Thinking he is the son of Polybus and Merope, he strives to avoid the pollution of parricide and incest by fleeing Corinth; as political leader of Thebes, he struggles to rid his city of the plague by tracking down the killer of Laius; and, when the opportunity arises, he applies his energies relentlessly to untangle the riddle of his own identity.

This last effort, the most compelling in the play, returns Oedipus to the riddle of the Sphinx on which his earlier fame rests. The answer to the question 'What creature goes on two, three, and four feet?' is man. Oedipus himself personifies the enigma, a tragic figure who is more than one (terrible) thing at a time. It is important to note that in his confusion Oedipus manifests no moral failing or 'tragic flaw', a (mis)translation of Aristotle's term *hamartia,* which literally implies an archer 'missing the mark', not hitting a bull's-eye. Oedipus errs through simple ignorance of the material facts of his own birth. Out of that situation Sophocles crafts a play that is both keenly particular (Oedipus is like no man) and broadly universal. Do any of us know who we really are, what we are doing, the full consequence of our actions?

The audience's familiarity with the story operates to best advantage in the play's ubiquitous ironies. As Oedipus drives towards the truth, he unwittingly participates in a remarkable series of puns, perhaps nowhere more striking than on his own name. Meaning 'swollen-footed', a reference to the pierced ankles he suffered when exposed as a child, 'Oedipus' contains the Greek word *oide* meaning 'I know', literally, 'I have seen'. The prophet Teiresias taunts Oedipus with 'not knowing who lives with you' (337–38), prompting the retort 'but I/the one who knows nothing, Oedipus, I stopped the Sphinx' (396–97). The verbal play, more prominent in the Greek than in most English translations, suggests that Oedipus' name signals his destiny. A man of intellect, whose rational gaze saw through the riddle of the Sphinx, gradually comes to realize how flawed his vision and understanding have been. His self-blinding adds further irony to his name, 'Oedipus—the one who has seen'.

—Rush Rehm, *Greek Tragic Theatre*. London and New York: Routledge (1992): pp. 109–10.

CHARLES SEGAL ON OEDIPUS REX AND THE MODERN READER

[Charles Segal is the author of *Aglaia: The Poetry of Alcman, Sappho, Pindar, Bacchylides, and Corinna* (1998) and *Euripides and the Poetics of Sorrow: Art, Gender and Commemoration in Alcestis, Hippolytus and Hecuba* (1993). In the excerpt below from his Introduction to *Oedipus Tyrannus,* Segal discusses the relevance of Sophocles' ancient story for the modern reader.]

The place of *Oedipus Tyrannus* in literature is something like that of the Mona Lisa in art. Everyone knows the story, the first detective story of Western literature; everyone who has read or seen it is drawn into its enigmas and moral dilemmas. It presents a kind of nightmare vision of a world suddenly turned upside down: a decent man discovers that he has unknowingly killed his father, married his mother, and had children by her. It is a story that, as Aristotle says in the *Poetics*, makes one shudder with horror and feel pity just on hearing it (14.1453b5–7). Tragedy stirs the deep emotions of pity and fear as it brings us face to face with suffering, strength, and courage at the outer limits of human experience; and *Oedipus* is Aristotle's favorite example for this tragic effect. We find the unexpected reversal in the lives of the great and fortunate deeply moving, both for individuals and for the state, as we know from contemporary responses to the deaths of famous people—our equivalent to the mythical kings of ancient Greece—such as that of Princess Diana of Britain. The stories of kings are themselves exemplary of the extreme limits of human criminality and human grandeur; and this play shows a great and passionate king confronting unspeakable horrors.

In Sophocles' hands this ancient tale also becomes a profound meditation on the questions of guilt and responsibility, the order (or disorder) of our world, and the nature of man. The play stands with the Book of Job, *Hamlet,* and *King Lear* as one of Western literature's most searching examinations of the problem of meaning and suffering. A life that seems happy, productive, and distinguished in the service of others suddenly crumbles into dust. The well-meaning king of Thebes—an effective, admired, and respected ruler—suddenly finds that he is not only the source of the calamity from which he has tried to protect his citizens, the plague with which the play begins, but also guilty of the two most horrible crimes imaginable: incest with his mother and the bloody killing of his father. The hero's determined march toward the horrifying discovery of these facts produces the feeling of an inexorable doom surrounding his life, as he recognizes that he has fulfilled prophecies that Apollo had given to him and his parents. In fact, the very attempts to avoid these prophecies seem to have brought them to pass. Thus, on one reading, the play is a tragedy of a destiny that the hero cannot evade, despite his best attempts to do so.

The play is a tragedy not only of destiny but also of personal identity: the search for the origins and meaning of our life, our balance between "one" and "many" selves, our recognition of the large areas of darkness about who we "really" are, and the effort to explore the essential mystery of our selfhood. It dramatizes the lonely path of self-discovery, as Oedipus separates his true self from an illusory self defined by the external status of his kingship, and retraces his existence from powerful ruler to lonely wanderer, without parents, city, home, or even a sure name. The hero chosen to perform exceptional deeds has also to undergo exceptional suffering as the polluted parricide and outcast who has infected his city.

—Charles Segal, Oedipus Tyrannus: *Tragic Heroism and the Limits of Knowledge.* New York and Oxford: Oxford University Press (2001): pp. 3–4.

◎

T. C. W. STINTON ON THE AUDIENCE IN ANCIENT GREECE

[T. C. W. Stinton is the author of *Euripides and the Judgment of Paris* (1965). In the excerpt below from the chapter entitled, "The Scope and Limits of Allusion in Greek Tragedy," Stinton discusses the audience of Greek tragedy and the extent to which a standard version of the Oedipus legend may be read into Sophocles work.]

The family curse of the Labdacids is seen by Lloyd-Jones to be a factor in *Oedipus Tyrannus* also. This enables him to accommodate the play to the scheme of divine justice whose ubiquity in early Greek thought is the theme of his book. For if Oedipus is under a curse inherited from his father, the crime that provoked the curse is the crime for which he is punished, this being, in archaic Greek thought as in Hebrew thought, conformable to divine justice. The difficulty with this interpretation is that neither the curse nor the crime of Laius is anywhere mentioned in this play, though there are several places where their mention would have been appropriate had they been important for Sophocles' purposes. Laius is said by Jocasta to have been told by the oracle of Apollo that he was fated to be killed by his son; therefore Oedipus was exposed at birth (711 ff.). The crime and the punishment must be those of another version of the legend, found in the lost *Chrysippus* of Euripides—probably that of the epic *Oedipodeia,* and, as we have seen, of the Oedipus trilogy of Aeschylus. But even if this was the standard version, Sophocles could hardly have made clearer his intention to diverge from it in this play. Lloyd-Jones maintains, however, that there are sufficient hints in the play to give the lead to an audience familiar with curses and used to obscure allusion:

> After the Theban slave has at last removed all doubts about
> his real identity, Oedipus prays that he may prove now to
> be looking for the last time upon the light of day—'I who
> am sprung', he says, 'from those who should not have
> begotten me, who am living with those I should not be
> living with, who have killed those whom I should not have
> killed' (1184–5). Why should Laius and Jocasta not have
> begotten Oedipus? The words have far more point if we
> recognise that Laius was warned beforehand.

The answer is that 'sprung from those I should not have been
sprung from' means that Oedipus' parents have turned out to be
those who should not have been his parents—the man he killed
and the woman he married. ⟨. . .⟩

⟨. . .⟩ This brings me to the question I set out to pose in this
paper. If a dramatist cannot omit a detail from the standard version of the legend without his audience filling it in for themselves,
how can he stop them filling in what he does not want filled in?
How can he ever depart from the standard form of a legend
without explicitly telling us where he is departing from it? It is of
course not always clear what is the 'standard version', whether it is
that of Homer or Aeschylus or the version represented in art or
presupposed in cult. There is in every legend a basic schema, which
cannot be altered without deforming the story. Thus the basic
schema or story-pattern of *Oedipus Tyrannus* is that Oedipus is a
foundling who unwittingly kills his father and marries his mother.
As Aristotle puts it (*Po.* 1453^{b}23–4), Clytemnestra has to be killed
by Orestes, Eriphyle by Alcmaeon; it is for the poet to vary the
story by adding to or rehandling its basic elements. Again, there
will often be trivial details we should not expect to become standard. So when in Oedipus no reason is given for Laius going to
Delphi (115), it is absurd to fill in the gap, with Jebb, by pointing
to Euripides' *Phoenissae* (36), where his motive is to enquire about
the exposed child; or to suggest, with Campbell, that a better
reason would be to enquire how to stop the ravages of the Sphinx;
or even to say, with Kamberbeek, that Sophocles must have had
a motive in mind but does not tell us what it was. The motive was
irrelevant, and to ask what it might have been is just a form of
the documentary fallacy. But between the essential schema and the
trivial detail there are also features of a story which acquire the

status of a standard version at a particular time, because they have general currency or because of the authority of the poets who have used them.

—T. C. W. Stinton, *Collected Papers on Greek Tragedy*. Oxford: Clarendon Press (1990): pp. 461–62, 464.

Cedric H. Whitman on Oedipus' Ill-Fated Quest for the Truth

[Cedric H. Whitman is the author of *Euripides and the Full Circle of Myth* (1974) and *The Heroic Paradox: Essays on Homer, Sophocles and Aristophanes* (1982). In the excerpt below from the chapter entitled "Irrational Evil: Oedipus Rex," Whitman attributes Oedipus' dilemma to his ill-fated quest to learn the truth.]

Oedipus was proverbial for two things—sagacity and atrocious misfortune. Greek popular wisdom had it that if a man were careful and prudent, he would avoid trouble. Of all men, Oedipus should have succeeded, but of all men he particularly did not. Oedipus remains a type of human ability condemned to destruction by an external insufficiency in life itself—as if knowledge were possible, but the objects of knowledge, to use Plato's phrase, were somehow illusory, or at least evil. Such is Oedipus in the Sophoclean version, and such he must have been always. The myth is ultimately its own best interpreter and needs no *fabula docet*. It is for form's sake alone that the *Oedipus Rex* closes with the same old Herodotean saw which opened the *Trachiniae*:

Let mortals hence be taught to look beyond
The present time, nor dare to say, a man
Is happy, till the last decisive hour
Shall close his life without the taste of woe. ⟨. . .⟩

For Sophocles, however, the tale has deeper though less clearcut implications. Something of the fiery character of Laius, as it is hinted at in the *Oedipus Rex*, is perhaps derived from Aeschylus. But Oedipus himself illustrated two great dilemmas: first, like Orestes, he was the unwilling instrument of crime, and second, he was at once the emblem of shrewd wisdom and utter blindness. Aeschylus must unquestionably have dealt with the first of these dilemmas, and it is probable that he believed that Oedipus, in some degree, deserved his sufferings. But it is with the second dilemma that Sophocles is concerned. In the *Oedipus Rex*, he passes over the question of whether or not Oedipus is morally guilty of parricide and incest and concentrates wholly on the extent of his knowledge. Later, in the *Oedipus at Colonus*, Sophocles reverted to the other dilemma, and made old Oedipus defend his moral innocence in several spirited harangues, but the whole matter of moral guilt or innocence is never broached, even for an instant, in the earlier play. Nevertheless, it can be demonstrated simply from the character of the king himself in the *Oedipus Rex*, that Sophocles never considered him morally guilty. He was, from the first, the man who contrived his own fall without deserving it. And to this bitter fact may be added the even bitterer one that the means by which Oedipus destroyed himself was not his folly but his keenly intelligent moral conscience, which led him to take every possible step to avoid the unspeakable pollution that had been prophesied for him.

As he tells us himself, Oedipus thought that he was the son of Polybus, King of Corinth; but once, after being twitted by a drunken companion about his origin, he consulted the oracle and was told that he was destined to kill his father and marry his mother. Horrified, he avoided his supposed parents thereafter and made his way through Phocis, where his real father, Laius, met and attacked him at a cross-roads. In the fight which ensued, Oedipus slew Laius and all but one of his companions, and then proceeded to Thebes. So far, if we make allowances for the bloody practices which travel in the wilder districts sometimes enjoined upon the wayfarer of the heroic age, Oedipus had behaved with a good conscience. At Thebes he found the "riddle-singing Sphinx," the pest of the land, which by his sagacity he destroyed. He was rewarded by the grateful citizens with the hand of the recently widowed queen, Jocasta. And so for some years he reigned and bred sons and daughters, a happy and revered ruler, until the coming of the plague, at which point Sophocles begins his play. The plague, we are told, had been sent as a punishment because the city was polluted by the unavenged blood of Laius. And now, apparently for the first time, the question arises: who is the murderer of Laius?

If Sophocles had wanted us to consider the problem of right and wrong, he would have dramatized the scene at the crossroads. Instead he has dramatized the search for the murderer; the whole action is therefore devoted to the effort to draw truth out of the uncertainty and ignorance which at first center around the plague and later begin to gather more and more ominously around the king himself.

—Cedric H. Whitman, *Sophocles: A Study of Heroic Humanism.* Cambridge, Mass.: Harvard University Press (1951): pp. 122–25.

Plot Summary of
Oedipus at Colonus

Produced around 409 B.C., Sophocles was almost ninety years old at the time he composed *Oedipus at Colonus.* It is, in fact, his last dramatic work and, therefore, his age easily provides a theoretical approach to the play. Secondly, the sense in Athens near the end of the Peloponnesian War was that the city, like the playwright, was running out of time. Furthermore, the reappearance of Oedipus, after a number of years since *Oedipus Rex,* was significant because it was the resurrection of the archetypal tragic man who again confronts his former antagonist, Creon, a man who has likewise grown old during the intervening years. It has been said by several scholars that this play is an eloquent expression of the concerns of senectitude, and it is interesting to note that while a body of town elders comprises the chorus in all three of the Theban plays, it is in *Oedipus at Colonus* that the elders refer so vividly and candidly to the hardships of growing old. And, in so doing, they exhibit their own feebleness in their inability to help Oedipus when assaulted by the Theban representative, and ineffectualness in the face of Creon's abduction of Antigone. Finally, the generational divide between Oedipus and Polynices further underscores the problems concomitant to old age, thereby making the case for an autobiographical interpretation of this play all the more compelling.

The mythical background of this play continues where *Oedipus Rex* ended. Oedipus' parricide and incest has been discovered and disclosed, and he has begged Creon to send him into exile. But, before doing this, Creon says that he must first consult with the Delphic Oracle to ascertain what Apollo has commanded. Oedipus had remained in Thebes for several years until Creon and other Thebans decided that his presence polluted the city and, therefore, that he must leave. However, though Oedipus at this point wants to remain in Thebes, there is no one to take his part, especially his two sons, Eteocles and Polynices. Instead they allow him to wander as a beggar, with only his two daughters, Antigone and Ismene, to look after him. Indeed, Antigone accompanies Oedipus during his wanderings, while the two sons vie for the throne of Thebes. As it turns out, Eteocles, with the help of Creon, succeeds in banishing Polynices. Polynices seeks refuge in Argos, where he marries Argeia and persuades her father, Adrastus, to wage war on Thebes. In the meantime, Oedipus and Antigone have found haven in the grove of the Eumenides, the Kindly Goddesses, at Colonus, a village near Athens.

The opening scene takes place before the grove of the Eumenides in Colonus, a small Attic deme (village) north of the Acropolis which was especially rich in sanctuaries of the gods, and where in 411 B.C. an assembly was held to vote democracy out of existence. Nevertheless, Sophocles had a great affection for its natural beauty. Led by his daughter, Antigone, the aged and blind beggar Oedipus stops to rest in the mouth of a grove, when a local Scout arrives, and orders them to leave that place, since it is sacred to the Eumenides, "the terrifying goddess-daughters of Earth and Darkness [who] own it." When he hears this, Oedipus refuses to move because he considers this to be his final resting-place. He later tells Antigone when they are alone, what Apollo had once prophesied: "When he predicted my many disasters, / he told me that they would stop eventually / when I reached a final resting-place, where / I would find a welcome from the holy gods / . . . bringing rewards to those receiving me / and ruin to those who shunned me." The Scout explains that Colonus is ruled by Theseus, son of Aigeus and king of Athens, whom Sophocles represents here as a strong and very honorable ruler, embodying the requisite characteristics of the Athenian notion of the ideal man. Oedipus asks him to summon the king to ask his permission to bless his burial ground. The Scout is unwilling to force Oedipus to leave and, instead, takes leave of Oedipus and Antigone to inform the villagers about the strange visitor, and allows them to decide whether he can remain in the sacred grove. Oedipus pleads with the Eumenides to receive him: "So grant me, / goddesses, according to Apollo's / prophecy an end, a final turning."

When the Chorus of Elders arrive at the sacred grove, they at first treat him with great suspicion because he is a stranger to their city, "You must not / trespass along the grassy bank / where silence rules, where libations / of water mixed with / honey are poured." And when they find out his true identity, they recoil from the awful realization and demand that Oedipus leave the sacred area before he speaks to them. "Deceit piled up against deceit . . . Go on—off that seat! Get out of here!" Reluctantly, as Antigone eloquently pleads for their understanding,—"you've heard / stories of his unintended action"—the Chorus of Elders allow Oedipus to speak. He comes forward to address them and argues powerfully and persuasively that they are obligated to offer a stranger sanctuary, at least until their ruler comes. "I've come devout, with reverence, to the / advantage of these citizens. And when / you're leader comes . . . then you will hear and understand. Meanwhile / don't treat me unjustly in any way." Moved by his passionate plea, the Chorus of Elders decides to defer to Theseus on the question of whether Oedipus will be permitted to remain.

Suddenly, Ismene arrives on a pony. After the joyful reunion, she brings Oedipus bad news from Thebes that Eteocles has deposed Polynices from the throne, and that Polynices is raising a foreign army to attack his own homeland. In Oedipus' poignant response to the love and sacrifice of his two daughters, he makes a sharp distinction between their heroic behavior and that of his two selfish and misguided sons and, further, in that comparison he sees a reversal of traditional gender roles. "My daughters, they should bear the brunt of this / but no, they do the housekeeping like girls, / and it's you not they who shoulder all my / miseries." Meanwhile, the Thebans have dispatched Creon to bring Oedipus back, not to live in the city, but to be present and then buried at the boundary line, in order that they may gain the prosperity promised by the oracles upon the death Oedipus. Ismene further reports to her father that the envoys of the Delphic oracle have revealed that Thebes will one day be oppressed by invoking Oedipus' anger towards this terrible injustice. Having heard this, Oedipus furiously denounces his sons when he learns that they are simply trying to comply with the oracles in order that they may gain the throne of Thebes. "Then let the gods not tame this strife that's been / ordained for them. . . . They didn't stop me or / prevent me being driven out from home, humiliated — / their own father!" Remembering this, Oedipus expresses his fervent wish that the gods not allow either of them to rule. "No joy in ruling Thebes will ever come / their way. I know this; I have heard / her oracle."

At the request of the Chorus of Elders, Ismene is sent to perform the rites of atonement to the Eumenides for Oedipus' earlier trespass upon their grove. "Make yourself clean now before these goddesses. / When you first came, you trespassed in their grave." As Oedipus is old and blinded, Ismene must perform the obeisances by fetching holy water, pouring it into specially crafted bowls and, in turn, pouring the libations three times while standing and facing east. The

Colonians then question Oedipus about his parricide and incest and Oedipus continues to defend himself earnestly, explaining that he was ignorant of his crimes at the time he committed them. "I've borne the worst disasters, sirs, borne / them / readily, God knows; / though none of them my choice."

When Theseus arrives, he is very kind and benevolent, welcoming Oedipus as a citizen of Thebes and immediately offering him help. "Tell me. You'd need to speak of an horrific act / indeed to make me turn away from you. I well recall my own youth spent in exile." He offers to take Oedipus home with him, although Oedipus declines, saying that he will master his opponents here. Theseus leaves and the Chorus sings an ode to Oedipus, telling him of the beauty and tranquility of the place he has come to. "Every day, beautiful sprays / of narcissus—the crown of the— / might goddesses of old— / bloom afresh in the heavenly / dew, with the golden crocus." But Creon soon arrives with some guards, and destroys the pleasing mood suggested by the ode. "People of Colonus. Noble residents. / Your eyes, I see, reflect some / sudden fear at my entrance." He invites Oedipus to come home, on behalf of all the Thebans, but Oedipus bitterly denounces Creon's dishonest and self-serving overtures. "I'll show your baseness—why / you've come to seize me; not to take me home, / but to the border so that Thebes will stay / unharmed, delivered from Athens itself." Creon then reveals to Oedipus that he has captured Ismene, and after a struggle, his guards abduct Antigone as well. However, Theseus returns, summoned from a sacrifice to Poseidon, the patron-god of Colonus, by the noise of this struggle, and as soon as he learns what has happened to Oedipus' daughters, he dispatches one of his servants to gather a crowd to liberate the girls. Theseus then proceeds to rebuke Creon for presuming that the Athenians would allow him to do this. "It wasn't Thebes who taught you to do wrong. / She hates to nurture men outside the law. / She'd not approve you if she heard you had / despoiled what's mine and— yes!—the gods', in seizing / helpless suppliants by force."

While Creon tries to defend his actions, Oedipus delivers a masterly counter-plea. "Shameless arrogance! What do you think / you insult now—my old age or your own? / The list of murder, marriage, accidents / you rattle off so readily I unfortunately had / to bear against my will. But it suited the gods. / . . . But you'd not find a thing to blame me for—on my own." Theseus then makes Creon lead him to where the girls are held captive while the Elders evoke the battle in song and dance. "He will be caught! Fearsome is our ally, Ares, / fearsome is the might of Theseus," following which song Theseus returns with Oedipus' daughters. Theseus tells Oedipus something he has just learned, namely that a relative of Oedipus has taken refuge at the altar of Poseidon, and wants an audience with Oedipus. Oedipus guesses that this relative is none other than Polynices, and when he finally grants his son an audience, upon the intercession of Theseus and an impassioned plea by Antigone, it is merely to curse him. "You'll never conquer Thebes / through civil war . . . You will die at the hand of your brother / and in turn kill him who banished you / I pray for this."

Polynices is quite disturbed by this curse and begs of Antigone that when he meets his inevitable fate, that she see to her brother's proper burial, with funeral gifts and praise. "This is the path / that I must take, doomed though it is and luckless / because of my father and his Furies. / May Zeus bless you if you do what I ask." Though Antigone continues to remonstrate with Polynices to abandon this hopeless attack on Thebes, he tells her he cannot call his comrades back from the road they have begun to pursue. Instead, Polynices leaves her brokenhearted with the knowledge that she will be the one to suffer from his loss.

As the Elders begin to sing another song about evil begetting evil, thunder breaks out. "Watch out! The mighty, awesome thunderbolt / of Zeus comes crashing down. Fear / makes my hair stand on end." Oedipus recognizes this as a sign that the gods are calling him, "[t]he winged thunder of Zeus will lead me / now / to Haides," and asks for Theseus to be brought back. Theseus comes, and gifted in his last moments with supernatural vision, Oedipus takes him to a secret place where he already knows he will die. "You must never show this place to any man / or say where it is hidden, where it lies . . . When you go there by yourself, you'll learn / mysteries which can never be spoken." In his final speech, he prophesies great benefits to Athens for receiving him if Theseus accepts his responsibility to hold these secrets sacred. "Guard them throughout your life, and when you come / to die, reveal them to one special elder . . . That way you'll live in Athens unmolested by / the Thebans." The Chorus prays for Oedipus' peace in the Underworld. "Oh earth's goddesses, oh the beast that can't be / conquered, . . . I pray most earnestly / to make the pathway clear when this / man comes into death's realm." A Messenger now enters to announce Oedipus' death. Antigone and Ismene return, grieving. For a few moments, Antigone wants to go back to her father's grave, but Theseus, who now returns, reminds her that she cannot. "Stop lamenting, girls. Now that / a benefit lies stored in the earth's dark night, / we must not grieve. For divine anger would follow." So she begs him to send her and Ismene back to Thebes, to try to prevent their brothers from bloodshed. Theseus agrees to grant her request, to do "anything in the / future which is for your good, and / respects him under the earth who has just / gone from us." ✿

List of Characters in
Oedipus at Colonus

Oedipus is the protagonist of *Oedipus Rex* and *Oedipus at Colonus*. Blind and feeble with age, he has been living in exile. He is determined to defend himself against the citizens of Colonus in order to make peace with the gods at his final resting place.

Antigone, daughter of Oedipus and Jocasta, takes care of her father in his old age.

The **Elders of Colonus** at first do not want Oedipus at their sacred grove and try to cast him out. However, they allow him to stay after Ismene performs the rights of atonement on his behalf.

Ismene, daughter of Oedipus and Jocasta, arrives in Colonus to visit her father and sister. She performs the rights of atonement for her father. Later in the play, she is captured by Creon but is released with the help of Theseus.

Theseus is the King of Athens in Oedipus at Colonus. He takes pity on Oedipus and defends him against Creon. In return his city is granted an enduring blessing.

Creon becomes the King of Thebes and banishes Oedipus. Authoritarian and stubborn, he is willing to fight with his nephews Eteocles and Polynices to keep control of the throne.

Polynices is the son of Oedipus. He arrives in Colonus to seek his father's blessing in his battle with his brother. Oedipus tells him that he will be cursed if he goes through with the battle, and his sister Antigone will be the one to suffer the consequences.

Eteocles is the youngest son of Oedipus who forces his brother Polynices out of Thebes. He battles Polynices for control of Thebes, which will result in the deaths of both brothers at each other's hand.
❀

Critical Views on
Oedipus at Colonus

P .E. EASTERLING ON THREE DOMINANT IMAGES

[P. E. Easterling is an editor of *Greek Religion and Society*
(1985) and *The Cambridge Companion to Greek Tragedy*
(1997). In the excerpt below from her article, "Plain Words
in Sophocles," Easterling discusses three dominant images
of Sophoclean language in *Oedipus at Colonus*.]

Writing a commentary on *Oedipus at Colonus* had made me think
about how to do justice to the extraordinary poise and power of
Sophoclean language, despite its seeming simplicity in this late play.
Hence, the 'plain words' of my title, but plain in the spirit of Shakespeare's Lear.

> Pray do not mock me.
> I am a very foolish fond old man
> Fourscore and upward, not an hour more or less;
> And, *to deal plainly,*
> I fear I am not in my perfect mind.
> Methinks I should know you and know this man;
> Yet I am doubtful: for I am mainly ignorant
> What place this is, and all the skill I have
> Remembers not these garments; nor do I know
> Where I did lodge last night. Do not laugh at me;
> For, as I am a man, I think this lady
> To be my child Cordelia.

> (*King Lear* IV. viii. 60–71)

What I mean by 'plain words' or 'dealing plainly' is not artless
naivety or homely colloquialism; I am well aware that Sophoclean
discourse—like Shakespeare's—is typically artful in the extreme,
relying on a range of vocabulary that includes many abstract nouns
and many synonyms, often coinages, whcih make possible an elaborate use of *variatio.* ⟨. . .⟩

What I am looking for is a way of analysing the concentration and power of this language without falling back on overworked terms like ambiguity, irony, undercutting, deferral.

There are three images, or models, that I have found useful in trying to account for the depth of Sophocles' plain dealing, though all, of course, are makeshift: (1) the notion of the tension of opposites, or the holding together of contradictory forces; (2) the idea of oscillation, or shading between literal and metaphorical meaning; (3) the idea of the 'charging' of themes through concentration and the ever-varied use of repetition. Rough and sketchy as they are, they have the advantage of not being mutually exclusive, and at least they should not run the risk of being reductive.

1. *Contradiction.* The strongest contradiction within this speech is that between the *magnitude* of Oedipus' experience ⟨. . .⟩ and the *smallness* of what he now asks for, receives and accepts. ⟨. . .⟩ As the play develops we shall find that strong emphasis is given to the question whether Oedipus' request to Theseus and the men of Colonus is *small* or *great,* and to the idea of the *little word* that can exert unexpected power for good or evil. But even at this stage the contrast between great and small is striking. The last word of his speech is worth noting, too: 'perform', 'fulfil', is a word of some dignity, often used of carrying out ritual, as at 513, when Ismene offers to perform the rite of purification, or of the action of gods, supernatural forces or time 'bringing things to pass', as in Oedipus' famous words after his self-blinding. ⟨. . .⟩ Not what a helpless beggar might be expected to say of himself and his daughter, not (that is) if he were not also Oedipus. ⟨. . .⟩ The speaker, of course, is not any old anonymous wanderer: like Antigone, he is a famous character of the tragic stage. The meaning of Oedipus' identity is going to be at the centre of the play's meditations; what, if anything, he can fulfil is going to matter.

2. *Shading from literal to metaphorical,* an extremely familiar feature in poetry ancient and modern, works particularly well in drama because everything in a play is in a sense metaphorical, in that it presents past and/or fictitious events *as if* they were happening here and now before the audience's eyes. When the audience watches Oedipus, the name can with equal propriety be used both of him as

a character in the story and of the actor playing the part. Movement between literal and metaphorical is thus very easy: the journey of Oedipus, symbolized by the actor's movements on the stage, can be both his journey to Colonus and his passage from life to death. ⟨. . .⟩

3. *'Charging'.* Everything I have mentioned so far turns out to belong to the set of strands or themes that are constantly reworked and elaborated as the action develops. These first thirteen lines introduce all the play's leading ideas: personal/social relationships (child, strangers and citizens); Oedipus as wanderer and exile, blind, old, dependent on others (although the scanty gifts that he receives will later be replaced by the gift of asylum and reciprocated by a great benefit to the Athenians, the protective gift of his body); the journey of Oedipus and his daughter; the place they have come to, which may be a city of men; the seat where Oedipus will sit (an unusual work marking an important feature of the setting, which will turn out to be a suppliant's seat); the question of hallowed or unhallowed ground that is, the religious meaning of the place where Oedipus establishes himself. Oedipus knows how to endure, he asks for little and is content with less, but has been taught by great things. He has been taught by his experiences, and yet he has come to learn and also to fulfil. Later he will be found to be a teacher, too.

—P. E. Easterling, *Sophocles Revisited,* Jasper Griffin, ed. Oxford and New York: Oxford University Press (1999): pp. 95–99.

⟨❦⟩

LOWELL EDMUNDS ON THE STAGING OF OEDIPUS' OPENING SPEECH

[Lowell Edmunds is the author of *Intertextuality and the Reading of Roman Poetry* (2001) and *Poet, Public and Performance in Ancient Greece* (1997). In the excerpt below from the chapter entitled "Theatrical Space in *Oedipus at Colonus*," Edmunds imagines the staging of Oedipus' opening speech.]

An old man and a young woman enter from the spectators' left, and slowly traverse the 100 feet or more from the corner of the Long Hall (if the beginning of their entrance is measured from this point) to the place on the stage where they will stop, short of the center. The stage is slightly raised above the orchestra, where the chorus will later enter, and, at the edge of the stage, there are two rocks, one closer to the left, the other closer to the right, which will be Oedipus' seats. The façade of the wooden stage building (*skênê*) in front of the Long Hall may or may not have had painted scenery representing the grove of the Eumenides; it had an opening into the interior of the grove. The slowness and difficulty of the man's gait indicate his age. His mask shows that he is blind (286; 551–56); his hair is wild and unkempt (1261). The two wear the tattered clothes of beggars (555, 747–51, 1258–60, 1597), and the old man carries a beggar's pouch (1262–63). The young woman leads him; he is so feeble that he cannot walk without support. It is a highly conventional scene: a child or an attendant leads a blind person on stage. As they proceed along the stage, the old man begins to speak, naming the young woman: "Child of a blind old man, Antigone, what region have we reached or what city of men?" (1–2). The old man's question breaks the convention by which the attendant is mute: this one is a named character who will be able to speak. He concludes by asking her to stop his movement and sit him down (11). She identifies the place as best she can, and then complies with his desire to be seated (14–20). The old man is so feeble that his sitting down is difficult and protracted (consider 19–22).

Oedipus' opening speech contains more than one kind of mimetic discourse. At the simplest level, "blind old man" refers to the figure seen by the spectators from the moment of its entrance and already identified as such visually; and "Antigone" (1) and "the wanderer Oedipus" (3) attach names to the two characters. But only in these matters of "factual" information can Oedipus' discourse be mimetic. Since he cannot see the stage space and the other characters, his discourse cannot refer to them, at least not as things perceived. Thus his discourse can never participate in the dramatic autoreflexivity of the other characters' discourse, which can always refer to the stage space that they and the spectators can see (cf. Chapter 1). Oedipus cannot, for example, use a demonstrative pronoun of someone or something on stage, unless the referent has been supplied to him (as, for the first time apropos of the stage space, at 45). His discourse can be mimetic only at a second remove, as mimetic of someone else's mimetic discourse. To return to the opening lines (1–2), the interrogative form of the sentence represents not only the character's desire for information but, more fundamentally, the fact that he is blind. His disjunction between "region" and "city of men" arises from his inability to make the perceptual distinction that would have simplified the question or rendered it unnecessary. Thus the interrogative form itself mimetizes the speaker's blindness and, in effect, announces Oedipus' whole relation to the stage space. His discourse can never be commensurate, in this respect, with that of the other characters. He can only refer to his own actions, and, since he depends upon others for guidance and support, these will tend to be stated in the form of questions, commands, refusals, and entreaties.

—Lowell Edmunds, *Theatrical Space and Historical Place in Sophocles'* Oedipus at Colonus. Lanham, Maryland, and London: Rowman & Littlefield Publishers, Inc. (1996): pp. 39–41.

CYNTHIA P. GARDINER ON THE CHORUS OF ELDERS

[Cynthia P. Gardiner is the author of *The Sophoclean Chorus: A Study of Character and Function.* In the excerpt below from the chapter entitled "*Antigone, Oedipus Tyrannus, Oedipus Coloneus*," Gardiner discusses some of the physical characteristics and function of the chorus of elders in *Oedipus at Colonus.*]

In *Oedipus Coloneus* we seem to have another chorus of civic elders subordinate to a king and we may perhaps expect them to perform one or another of the political functions for which the Theban Elders were used. Certainly they are far more involved in the structure of the drama than the chorus of *Antigone;* and even the chorus of *Oedipus Tyrannus* do not have half the number of kommoi that the poet has given to the Elders of Colonus. ⟨...⟩

The rich structural variety and the unusually large number, for Sophocles, of the chorus' utterances are concomitant with a character that is suitably complex and yet as transparent as any in the extant plays of this poet. The chorus' entrance is prepared by two items of information. First, the Stranger's explanations prepare the audience to assume that the members of the chorus, although governed by Athens (67), are not residents of the city of Athens (78), but are local inhabitants, the namesakes of the local divinity Colonus (58–65), who have at least some autonomy of decision (79–80). Then Antigone remarks when she sees them approaching that they are old men (111–112). Their advanced age is stressed again and again in the play and would therefore probably be evident in their appearance. The chorus' costume would also immediately identify for the audience another aspect of their persona that is later indicated by the text: they are not simple peasants but well-born locals (728); in fact, the "Lords of the land" (831). We may wonder whether, among other reasons, Sophocles chose to set the play in Colonus so that he might have such a chorus of elderly "gentry" without introducing the politically awkward concept of a feudal nobility in democratic Athens (and perhaps also because a kidnapping could not reasonably be supposed to occur within the city of Athens itself).

These are the basic physical aspects of the chorus' role that are apparent even before they speak. Next, in the parodos (117ff.), the poet presents important aspects of their personality, the first of which is their piety. They enter with a strong tone of hostility, but their hostility is directed against Oedipus as the reputed desecrater of a holy place, so holy that they themselves customarily avert their eyes in silence as they pass it (125–133). The initial tension created by these jealous defenders of sanctity is, however, abated by their compassion, for as soon as they perceive Oedipus' blindness, they pity him (150–152) and offer to help him avoid religious pollution (153–154). This balance of piety and compassion in their character is carefully maintained; they are not religious bigots, but rather honest men faced with a choice between holiness and kindness. Although they firmly promise, out of compassion and a sense of justice, that no one will ever drive Oedipus away from the place (174–177), Sophocles places them in the moral dilemma of having to order him away at once when they learn his identity, lest he pollute the land (226–236). Then Antigone's passionate plea causes them to weaken in their resolve and to admit their perplexity honestly ⟨. . .⟩ (254–257). They are reasonable men: when Oedipus argues that to turn him away would be in itself an impiety (276–277), they are content to resolve their conflict by referring it to higher authorities (292–295).

But the poet does not end here the chorus' involvement in this problem. They witness the meeting of Ismene and Oedipus, they hear Ismene's news of events in Thebes and the new oracles, they hear Oedipus' tale of suffering at the hands of his own sons. When he appeals to them at the end of this series of woes (457–460), they are again moved by compassion and offer him the help of religion, to appease the deities whose sanctuary he violated. The subsequent description of the ritual that must be performed, which has often been called irrelevant, is most impressive when viewed in proper dramatic context. The chorus' piety and reverent conduct have been heavily stressed in the play thus far; now they behave as knowledgeable priests, directing each detail of the sacrifice with solemn imperatives and framing the great prayer to the Eumenides for safety (486–487).

—Cynthia P. Gardiner, *The Sophoclean Chorus: A Study of Character and Function.* Iowa City: University of Iowa Press (1987): pp. 109–11.

G. O. Hutchinson on the Meaning of Oedipus' Journey

[G. O. Hutchinson is the author of *Cicero's Correspondence: A Literary Study* (1998) and *Hellenistic Poetry* (1988). In the excerpt below from his essay, "Sophocles and Time," Hutchinson discusses the contrast between Oedipus' experience of continuous wandering with the fixity of place which marks the completion of his journey and the greater significance of his death.]

This paper is not directly concerned with Sophocles' views on time. It is interested rather in considering how structures of time are used in the plays to shape the experiences they depict and provide. In a literary work time is, among other things, a way of organizing material, articulating its meaning, intensifying its force. The sequence of past, present, and future is a framework fundamental to most criticism of drama; but the area of time that will primarily concern us here is the opposition, little explored for drama, between imperfective and perfective. ⟨. . .⟩ Can we sharpen our understanding of the tragedies by considering a contrast between (roughly) single, decisive, final events, and continuous states or repeated attempts, which fall short of, or look towards, completion and fulfilment? ⟨. . .⟩

Two of the plays with male central figures are similarly founded on the long period of suffering which the foremost character has endured: the *Philoctetes* and the *OC*. The exigencies of space allow only a discussion of the latter, and that a brief one. The *OC* is chosen because it is particularly rich and intricate in its use of 'aspect', as of time in general; it should be evident enough that the kind of analysis applied above to the *Electra* and the *Trachiniae* can fruitfully be applied to the *Philoctetes*.

The *OC*, like the other three plays, is built around an extended, imperfective experience which leads up to the present; what is built around it is particularly elaborate. The experience is that of Oedipus' life of exile as a wandering beggar. The idea of wandering is much stressed, though little is said of particular places Oedipus has passed through (compare Walcott's *Omeros*!). By contrast with the fixity of Philoctetes or Electra, Oedipus' experience is defined by unresting motion. The present place as well as the present time are set against this incessant movement. Oedipus will here be received, fixed, and will not move; his wanderings and his life will end. ⟨. . .⟩ With that conception are swiftly associated repeated begging, poverty, acceptance, heroic endurance, prolonged life; the idea of extended time is soon explicitly added (22). Ironically Oedipus sees in ⟨this day⟩ (3–4) mere repetition of a routine, varied in place but not substance; in fact the present day will provide the perfective end to that routine. The visual side of the opening is no less important: the slow movement, guided by Antigone, which embodies the wandering, and their squalid appearance, which embodies his degraded exile.

Later, when Oedipus speaks of Antigone's life, he conveys in an expressively long sentence the extension of what she has undergone, and the poverty. (345–52) ⟨. . .⟩

Most fundamentally, the play sets the supreme event of the play, Oedipus' death, against the long time which has preceded it. The shape is already set out plainly, with the authority of an oracle, at the start of the play. ⟨. . .⟩

The moment itself, the death, is heralded at the end of the play by thunder; this thunder appears for the moment to sweep away all the entanglements of sons and Thebans. It was forecast as a sign in the prologue (94–5); characteristically, this event itself seems less perfective when experienced in stage time: the terrifying sound and sight occur repeatedly. But the decisiveness of the happening is clear, and its meaning as bringing an end to Oedipus' life (1460–1, 1472–3, etc.). The speed and resolution with which Oedipus himself now guides the others, following the god, eerily marks a contrast with the movement at the beginning of the play, and with the life he is now ending (1551–2).

In a speech to his daughters reported by the messenger Oedipus proclaims that 'this day' (1612) sees the end of his life, and of their labours in looking after him. As hitherto, the girls' sufferings are partly a way of talking about Oedipus' sufferings, but are partly distinct. The speech ends in a potent contrast with its beginning: Oedipus will end his life, and so the girls their toil; but they will live on, unlike him, and spend the rest of their lives mourning for him.

—G. O. Hutchinson, *Sophocles Revisited,* Jasper Griffin, ed. Oxford and New York: Oxford University Press (1999): pp. 47, 58–61.

☙

BERNARD KNOX ON THE HISTORICAL BACKGROUND

[Bernard Knox is the author of *Word and Action: Essays on the Ancient Theater* (1979) and *Essays Ancient and Modern* (1989). In the excerpt below, from the chapter entitled "Oedipus at Colonus," Knox discusses the play in the context of the historical circumstances of Sophocles life during the time in which he wrote the play, emphasizing the simultaneous death of Oedipus and Athens.]

It is the last play, written just before the poet's death, and not performed until five years after it. He died in 406 B.C., two years before the destruction of the Athenian fleet at Aegospotami; he did not live to see the Spartan galleys, their oarsmen paid by Persian subsidies, sail into the Piraeus and force the surrender of Athens. But he knew already, as all the world must have known, that Athens had lost the war, that it faced certain defeat and, possibly—so greatly was Athens hated—extinction. In the last terrible years of mounting despair, the dream of the Funeral Speech had turned into a nightmare. The government of the democracy was in the hands of violent, ignorant demagogues, the Attic soil beleaguered by a Spartan garrison at Decelea, a short day's march from Athens, the flower of Athenian manhood lost in Sicily and a score of indecisive battles on the Aegean. In the last months of his long life, Sophocles, born in the village of Colonus ninety years before, turned back to the figure of Oedipus, whom he had once portrayed as the ideal type of Athenian intelligence and daring, and wrote this strange play about the hero's old age, about the recompense he received for his sufferings, and also about Athens.

The recompense Oedipus is to receive is death—death as a human being, but power and immortality as something more than human, in fact as a protecting hero of the Attic soil. The close association of Oedipus with Athens is full of significance. Oedipus *tyrannos* was the Athenian ideal of the days of the city's greatness, but his courage, energy, and intelligence were set in a tragic framework where their heroic impetus brought about his fall. The old Oedipus of this play is like the exhausted, battered Athens of the last years of the war, which, though it may be defeated and may even be physically destroyed, will still flourish in immortal strength, conferring power on those who love it. It is no coincidence that this play contains the most moving and beautiful ode in praise of Athens that was ever written, a poem which celebrates Athens' strength, power, and beauty in images which suggest death and immortality in the same breath. The city, like Oedipus, may die, but only to become immortal.

The play is a worthy last will and testament. All the great themes of the earlier plays recur; it is as if Sophocles were summing up a lifetime of thought and feeling in this demonic work of his old age. The blind man who sees more clearly than those who have eyes is now not the prophet Tiresias but Oedipus himself, who prophesies, first in the name of Apollo and then in his own. As in the *Oedipus Tyrannus* and *Trachiniae*, the action unrolls against the background of the oracular prophecies of the gods, those cryptic, partial revelations of the divine knowledge which the human intellect cannot accept or understand until they are fulfilled. 〈. . .〉 And death, that death Ajax and Antigone proudly claimed as their own, which Electra and Oedipus at Thebes wished for in their moments of despair, which Philoctetes preferred to the life among men which he had come, with good reason, to fear—that death is Oedipus' declared goal from the first: he is a wanderer looking for the place where it awaits him, his promised rest.

—Bernard Knox, *The Heroic Temper: Studies in Sophoclean Tragedy.*
Berkeley and Los Angeles: University of California Press (1998): pp. 143–45.

〈◉〉

PETER L. RUDNYTSKY ON *OC* AND ITS CONNECTION WITH THE OEDIPAL CYCLE

[Peter L. Rudnytsky is the author of *Contending Kingdoms: Historical, Psychological, and Feminist Approaches to the Literature of Sixteenth-Century England and France* (1991) and *The Psychoanalytic Vocation: Rank, Winnicott and the Legacy of Freud* (1991). In the excerpt below, from the chapter entitled "Incest and Burial," Rudnytsky focuses on *Oedipus at Colonus* to demonstrate its connection with the other two plays comprising the Oedipus cycle.]

Any study of the interrelations among Sophocles' Theban plays must begin with the recognition that they do not form a trilogy. *Antigone*, the earliest in order of composition, was probably produced in 442 B.C. and *Oedipus the King* in about 425 during the plague in the second year of the Peloponnesian War; *Oedipus at Colonus*, written shortly before Sophocles' death at the age of ninety in 406, was first performed posthumously in 402. The difficulties of interpretation are compounded by the fact that nothing certain is known about the other two works that were performed together with each of these plays, and which may or may not have been related to them in subject matter. It must be borne in mind, furthermore, that all three plays are independent wholes, apart from their relations to any larger sequence.

These important considerations notwithstanding, I wish to press the case for the unity of the Oedipus cycle. Certainly there are minor inconsistencies from one play to the next. ⟨. . .⟩

But these discrepancies are outweighed by the evidence for continuities linking the three plays. In *Oedipus at Colonus,* above all, it is clear that Sophocles has sought to establish connections with *Oedipus the King.* In a broad sense, the plot of *Oedipus at Colonus* constitutes a reversal and an undoing of the earlier play: instead of a movement from strength and weakness, there is movement from weakness to strength; and Oedipus, rather than attempting to circumvent the predictions of oracles, now aligns himself with the forces seeking their fulfillment. The parallels between *Oedipus the King* and *Oedipus at Colonus* are announced as early as the first word, since the address of the aged Oedipus to his daughter Antigone, *teknon* ("child"), recalls that of the proud king to his assembled people, *tekna* ("children"). The speeches of Oedipus opening both plays, moreover, are each thirteen lines long, and divided into units of eight and five lines, marked by the transition *alla* ("but"). Most significantly, Sophocles in *Oedipus at Colonus* has Oedipus allude (ll. 87–95) to his visit to the Delphic oracle recounted in *Oedipus the King* (ll. 788–93), where it had been foretold that he would kill his father and marry his mother, only Oedipus now discloses for the first time a new aspect of the prophecy—that he would find his final resting place in a grove of the Furies, whence he would become a blessing to his friends and a curse to his enemies. This direct reference to *Oedipus the King* in *Oedipus at Colonus,* and the transposition of Oedipus' fate into a new register, epitomizes the continuity between the two plays. Finally, it is noteworthy that in *Oedipus at Colonus* Sophocles attempts to smooth over the previous discrepancies in the accounts of the succession to the Theban throne, since Ismene explains (ll. 367–73) that the two sons—who, after all, were young boys at the time of Oedipus' fall—agreed *at first* to resign the throne to Creon, only to change their minds and battle with one another as they grew older. Whether one judges Sophocles' effort to obtain coherence to be skillful or maladroit is less important that the fact that he makes it at all, because the very undertaking shows his desire to preserve the unity of the Oedipus cycle. ⟨...⟩

⟨...⟩ It follows that the pivotal play in any discussion of the Oedipus cycle as a whole is *Antigone*, since it may be regarded either as a beginning or an ending. A further corollary is that the Oedipus cycle possesses *two* endings—*Antigone* and *Oedipus at Colonus*—which qualify and react upon one another. Recast in more theoretical terms, the implication of the double arrangement of the Theban plays is that they invite a reading that is at once *synchronic* and *diachronic.*

> —Peter L. Rudnytsky, *Freud and Oedipus.* New York: Columbia University Press (1987): pp. 275–77.

CHARLES SEGAL ON THE OUTCAST AND REINTEGRATION INTO SOCIETY

[Charles Segal is the author of *Aglaia: The Poetry of Alcman, Sappho, Pindar, Bacchylides, and Corinna* (1998) and *Euripides and the Poetics of Sorrow: Art, Gender and Commemoration in Alcestis, Hippolytus and Hecuba* (1993). In the excerpt below, from the chapter entitled "*Oedipus at Colonus:* The End of a Vision," Segal discusses some aspects of a new image of civilization and the outcast's reintegration into society.]

In the three late plays, *Electra, Philoctetes,* and *Oedipus at Colonus,* personal relationships play a crucial role in articulating a new image of civilization. The *Philoctetes* and the *Coloneus* treat an outcast's reintegration into society. As Philoctetes needs to separate himself emotionally from the hatred of his past and accept a present friendship that reaches back to the health of his pre-Odyssean and pre-Trojan self, so Oedipus must separate himself from the city of his embittered past, with its feuds and curses, and accept friendship and trust in a new city. Forcibly dragged back toward the old city of violence and pollution, Thebes, he chooses the enlightened piety of Athens. The contrast between the two cities and the two images of society that they embody is essential to an understanding of this play.

The *Oedipus at Colonus* begins, in a sense, where the *Philoctetes* leaves off. Instead of struggling against the all-ruling divinity of his destiny (*Phil.* 1467–68), Oedipus foreknows and accepts that destiny from the beginning. Like Philoctetes, he has the savagery of his anger, but he also possesses initially the *philia* that forms the inward and personal basis for his return to society. This outcast is not alone. He has with him the companion of his wanderings, Antigone. She is the child of the accursed marriage which drove him from Thebes but also the sign of his continuing bond with humanity. If his past has maimed him, it has also given him a support for those wounds. This support is not Philoctetes' magical weapon of a remote and now divinized hero but a frail human being whom he loves. She is the extension of that part of himself which can reach out to others. Thus she attends his crucial passage back into society and gives that saving counsel about listening and yielding (170–173) which the intransigent Philoctetes can receive from no mortal companion. The question for Oedipus is not, as it is for Philoctetes, whether he can be restored to civilization at all, but rather what kind of society can admit him.

Oedipus is an awesome, forbidding figure. His very appearance awakens the fear of pollution and touches off hard thoughts about the hidden workings of the gods. Only the city that is able to receive him and offer him shelter can also receive the mysterious blessings which he brings.

Set on its deserted island, the *Philoctetes* starts from a zero point of civilized values from which the two protagonists will have to rebuild a basis for human association. The *Coloneus* begins with the prospect of a towered city, approached through solemn, venerated places of great antiquity. The private microcosm of a heroic society realized between Philoctetes and Neoptolemus here expands to a full-fledged depiction of civil life under a noble leader, a society worthy of Oedipus' greatness. Unlike Heracles at the end of the *Trachiniae*, Oedipus' call from the gods at the end gives him a place at least partially within the framework of the polis.

Oedipus' return to society is also immersed in a setting of house and family. The bond of father and son provides a model for the association of Philoctetes and Neoptolemus; yet, despite the allusions to Philoctetes' home in Malis, family life is remote. The *Oedipus at Colonus,* however, deals directly with the interactions and tensions of a close-knit *oikos:* the loyalties of daughters, the neglect by sons, the anger of a father. The division of the son-archetype into two figures, Polyneices and Theseus, the accursed and the pious son, in turn reveals two aspects of the father, the angry patriarchal father who calls down the wrath of the gods of his house, and the generous, grateful father whose blessings bring continuity and security.

If the theme of accepting an outcast into the city links the *Coloneus* with the *Philoctetes,* the theme of the family curse links it with the *Electra.* The two works are in some ways mirror images of one another. In the *Coloneus* a polluted wanderer from outside the city frees himself from his curse when he enters a city and bestows on it his mysterious strength and blessing. In the *Electra* a figure coming from outside brings hope of release but also evokes the dark, continuing curses of the past (*El.* 1493ff.) and certainly does not confirm the city in its civilizing power with the clarity with which Oedipus' alliance with Theseus does. Whereas the *Electra* presents a disrupted mediation between man and god and between city and nature, the hero of the *Coloneus* is himself a powerful mediator between the city and the gods and between Olympian and chthonic divinity.

—Charles Segal, *Tragedy and Civilization: An Interpretation of Sophocles.* Cambridge, Massachusetts, and London: Harvard University Press (1981): pp. 362–63.

ROGER TRAVIS ON THE AUTHORITY OF THE CHORUS

[Roger Travis is the author of *Allegory and the Tragic Chorus in Sophocles' Oedipus at Colonus.* In the excerpt below, from the chapter entitled "From End to Beginning: The Choral Allegory of *Oedipus at Colonus*" Travis discusses the authority of the chorus in its exclusive power to end the tragedy.]

THE TRAGIC ENDING:

CHORAL UTTERANCE AND DRAMATIC CLOSURE

This discussion of *Oedipus at Colonus* begins by asking why. Why do the chorus alone have the power to end a tragedy? The sheer universality of choral closure can cause us to overlook the peculiar force of these final lines, to forget that in alone having the power to end the tragedy the chorus take for themselves a unique authority over the drama and the theatre. They claim power here both over the dramatic action of what we might call the *fabula* of *Oedipus at Colonus* and over the festival action of the tragic theatre, ending the play both for the characters and for the participants—themselves, the actors, and the spectators in the theatre. To question the convention of choral closure may seem ridiculous at face value, but the very multiplicity of tragic choral closures conceals an essential characteristic of the tragic theatre. Each final choral utterance ends a specific tragedy in a specific way, and in every one the chorus alone have the power to end the drama. From the "interior" of the drama, the chorus's final commands to the characters on stage carry a specific weight that derives not only from the convention of the choral ending but also from the particular status of their particular words. Moreover, this particular choral utterance performs a specific function; the chorus do not say something general about the gifts of the gods, nor do they say that the grief of the drama will continue, as we might in fact expect knowing what the next stage of the story holds: rather in their "soothing" way the chorus firmly take the drama out of the hands of the characters and into their own hands, making themselves the representatives of the *kuros* (authority) of the tragic theatre.

Specifically, the chorus here end the tragedy by curtailing the action of mourning simultaneously with the action of the drama. The immediate force of the chorus's final words serves to set a limit to the *thrênos* (dirge), to regulate it. The chorus accomplish this regulation by virtue of their conventional status as the representatives of the theatrical tradition of lyric verse, and their curtailment thus operates on several levels. Most obviously, their statement declares that the mourning suffices for the situation—Oedipus has reached a resolution and need not be mourned after the close of the present action. This immediate function makes sense of the contrast of these lines with the choral statements at the end of *Oedipus the King* and *Antigone,* both of which urge the reversibility of fortune: here Oedipus has gone beyond that reversibility and need no longer be mourned.

At the same time, though less immediately, the curtailment of mourning must also remind us of those Athenian laws that regulated mourning, especially the mourning of women. *Tad' ekhei kuros* "these present things have authority" expresses not only the validity of the preceding action, but also the invalidity of proceeding farther with the *thrênos.* Excess mourning works to threaten the stability of the obvious meaning of the choral imperatives that I glossed above: too much grief would demonstrate the insufficiency of the final resolution. The sumptuary laws serve to regulate display, to ensure that the polis does not waste itself in mourning and does not involve its elite members in factional rivalry; the chorus of *Oedipus at Colonus* make sure that the daughters of Oedipus do not waste the resolution of the tragedy, so favorable toward Colonus and Athens, in the expense of the *thrênos.* ⟨. . .⟩

⟨. . .⟩ To continue past the appointed end of *Oedipus at Colonus* would be to circle back to an earlier play, and a play that does not end with *kuros* but rather with basic uncertainty. The chorus of *Oedipus at Colonus* affirm the sufficiency of the action of *Oedipus at Colonus* to itself by denying the need for further drama. The demonstrative force of *tade* "these present things" works effectively to distinguish the present tragedy from the others that here at the close threaten to intrude: *these* things have validity, and not any others.

—Roger Travis, *Allegory and the Tragic Chorus in Sophocles'* Oedipus at Colonus. Lanham, Maryland, and London: Rowman & Littlefield Publishers, Inc. (1999): pp. 37–40.

☙

BERNARD WILLIAMS ON RESPONSIBILITY IN *OEDIPUS AT COLONUS*

[Bernard Williams is the author of *Censorship in a Borderless World* (1996) and *Meditations on First Philosophy*

(1996). In the excerpt below from his book, *Shame and Necessity,* Williams discusses the issue of responsibility of the unwitting agent in *Oedipus at Colonus.*]

So far we have been concerned with responses that are demanded by some people, or by a legal system, of other people. But there is another aspect to responsibility, which comes out if we start on the question not from the response that the public or the state or the neighbours or the damaged parties demand of the agent, but from what the agent demands of himself. Here we must turn back again from law and philosophy to tragedy, from the accident in the gymnasium to the mistake at the crossroads.

Oedipus's response, when he made his discovery, was self-imposed: "I have done it with my own hand," he says of his blinding. In the later play, he says that he afterwards came to think that what he had inflicted on himself was excessive. He also, at Colonus, says that he did not really *do* the things for which he blinded himself—and in a notably compacted expression: "I suffered those deeds more than I acted them." "Strained language," a progressivist critic writes, who sees these words as an overtaxed attempt to accommodate language to the kinds of considerations that appear in the *Tetralogies.* I doubt whether Sophocles was struggling to accommodate himself to the growth of the moral consciousness, and I am sure that if he merely wanted to describe what Oedipus did, he had adequate language to do so. What these words express is something much harder: Oedipus's attempt to come to terms with what his *erga,* his deeds, have meant for his life. For what, if one can ask a very ingenuous question, is one supposed to do if one discovers that not just in fantasy but in life one has murdered one's father and married one's mother? Not even Oedipus, as he is represented in his last days, thought that blinding and exile had to be the response. But should there be no response? Is it as though it had never happened? Or rather, to put the right question: Is it as though such things had happened, but not by his agency—that Laius had died, for instance, indeed been killed, but, as Oedipus first believed and then, for a short while, hoped, by someone else? ⟨. . .⟩

We have already seen that you can be held responsible by others for what you did unintentionally. Those who have been hurt need a response; simply what has happened to them may give them a right to seek it, and where can they look more appropriately than to you, the cause? In the modern world, for some such claims, you may have insurance, but a structure of insurance itself implies that the victims are looking in your direction. Moreover, not every claim, even now, is of a kind that could be met by insurance. Apart from your effects on other people, however, and your attitude to their lives, there is the question of your attitude to your own. Someone may simply have ruined his life, or, if he will not let anything make such an absolute determination of it, at least he may have brought it to a state of dereliction from which large initiatives and a lot of luck would be needed to get it back to anything worth having. If that has happened, then it is something that has happened to him, but at the same time it may be something that he has brought about. *What has happened to him, in fact, is that he has brought it about.* That is the point of Oedipus's words at Colonus. The terrible thing that happened to him, through no fault of his own, was that he did those things. ⟨. . .⟩

How much has been changed by what he did: that he was triumphantly king of Thebes, for instance, and now is not. Or what he himself now thinks about it; and one of the finest features of the *Oedipus at Colonus* is the way in which this embittered, helpless, and still angry man affects others with his own picture of his life.

—Bernard Williams, *Shame and Necessity.* Berkeley and Los Angeles: University of California Press (1993): pp. 68–71.

Plot Summary of
Antigone

A tragedy probably produced in 442 B.C. which, although it deals in part with the saga of Thebes, is subsequent to the action of *Oedipus Rex* and *Oedipus Colonus* and is the earliest written play of the three under consideration in this volume. It is a tragedy which begins with two figures assuming heroic postures, Antigone and Creon, but concludes with only one true exemplary character, its heroine, Antigone, proclaiming that "[n]o suffering of mine will be enough / to make me die ignobly." Although the play encompasses many issues concerning religion, politics, divided loyalties, the concerns of the present world versus the legacy of one's deeds after death, and gender roles in public life, the primary theme of *Antigone* is the conflict between private conscience and public duty. Creon (whose name means ruler) has issued an edict forbidding anyone to bury and mourn the body of the traitor, Polynices, whom he refers to as a "returned exile, / who sought to burn with fire from top to bottom / his native city." It is Creon's determination that Polynices' corpse should be left to rot on the ground, "to be chewed up by birds and dogs and violated." Indeed, anyone caught violating his edict is to be put to death by stoning, as Ismene (who is named after one of the rivers of Thebes) explains to her sister in the very beginning of the play. "Would you bury him, when it is forbidden by the city?" Nevertheless, Antigone, whose name literally means "opposed to offspring," is steadfast and brave in her determination to give her brother a proper burial. "I shall be / a criminal—but a religious one. The time in which I must please those that are dead / is longer than I must please those of this world. For there I shall lie forever." It should also be understood that the proper disposal of the dead was a fundamental right in classical Greece, extending as far as one's enemies as well. As such, a violation of this sacred right by any human being was destined to exact a terrible price by the gods. Upon the discovery that Antigone has indeed buried her brother, she is arrested and brought before Creon. Though she defends her actions, Creon decrees that she is to be imprisoned in a tomb and left to die. Moreover, there is a further predicament in deciding Antigone's fate as she is engaged to Creon's son, Haemon. But even Haemon's eloquent plea for the life of his beloved Antigone carries no weight with

Creon. Though Haemon advises his father "[t]hat that keeps the sheet of his sail too tight / and never slackens capsizes the boat," the tyrannical Creon will hear none of it. In the end, with both Antigone and Eurydice dead, Creon accepts the terrible fate which he has wrought upon himself. "Everything in my hands is crossed. A most unwelcome fate / has leaped upon me."

The tragedy is also enhanced by several magnificent choral odes. Indeed, it is the Chorus that provides the most beautiful and moving poetic commentary on the horrific events unfolding before its eyes. To mention just two examples of the Chorus' response to the terrible judgment and punishment which Creon places on Antigone as it poignantly expresses the utter loss of hope for the young woman: "Here was the light of hope stretched / over the last roots of Oedipus' house, / and the bloody dust due to the gods below / has mowed it down — that and the folly of speech / and ruin's enchantment of the mind." Elsewhere, in response to Creon's disavowal of his son's love for the young woman, the Chorus explains that love cannot be destroyed despite all attempts at its destruction. "You wrench the minds of just men to injustice, / to their disgrace; this conflict among kinsmen / it is you who stirred to turmoil . . . Love shares the throne with the great powers that rule. For the golden Aphrodite holds her play there / and then no one can overcome her."

As to the history of Thebes, it is a place located on the south edge of the eastern pain of Boeotia, and has been one the major settlements of Greece since the early Bronze Age. It was also the birthplace of Heracles who, as its champion, threw off the tribute levied upon it by the king of Orchomenus. By the late 6th century, Thebes had organized an alliance, a loose confederacy consisting of its neighbors, which excluded Orchomenus, and vied for control of all Boeotia. While it maintained friendly relations with some, it was hostile to Athens over the city of Plataea. In the ensuing battle, one group of Thebans stood with the other Greeks at Thermopylae, while another group of Thebans were in opposition. The Greek victory at Plataea in 479 B.C. led to their temporary assumption of power. Though Thebes allied itself with Sparta in 457 B.C, it was overwhelmed by an Athenian counterattack later that year. After a period of Athenian domination, the Boeotians again revolted against Athens and won the battle at Coronea in 447 B.C. Thereafter, Thebes was instrumental in instigating the Peloponnesian War by attacking Plataea in a time of peace. After the Theban defeat of Athens, it became estranged from Sparta and offered sanctuary to Athenian exiles hostile to the Thirty Tyrants, the Athenian oligarchs who had previously been granted political and legislative authority by the Spartans.

With respect to the degree of historical fact in Sophocles' story of *Antigone,* it is held by scholars that while Antigone is not purely an invented story, there is no concrete evidence concerning her earlier history. Indeed, there are various possible sources for Antigone's character. They are: (1) an epic entitled *Oedipodeia* in which Oedipus has four children by a woman named Euryganeia; (2) a fragment by Mimnermus which tells a story about Ismene; (3) a play by Aeschylus entitled *The Seven Against Thebes* which concludes with Antigone and Ismene mourning their brothers and Antigone defying an edict against burying Polynices. Nevertheless, here, the role of the two sisters is thought to be a spurious addition to the play, possibly influenced by Sophocles and Euripides' *Phoenissae;* (4) a dithyramb (a choral song in honor of Dionysus) by Ion of Chios in which Antigone and Ismene are burned to death in the temple of Hera, although it is uncertain whether this pre-dates Sophocles' play; (5) Pausanias, a periegetic writer of the extant *Description of Greece,* who claims to have been shown the place at Thebes where Antigone supposedly dragged the body of Polynices; and (6) Euripides' *Antigone* in which Antigone has a son, Maion, by Haemon.

Finally, as to other literary influences on Sophocles' *Antigone,* there is an epic, entitled *Thebais,* that tells the story of a blinded Oedipus who twice cursed his sons, Polynices and Eteocles, and prophesied that they would kill each other during a quarrel over their patrimony. The epic goes on to describe the Theban War, with the two brothers quarreling over the throne of Thebes and how Eteocles, the younger of the two, sent Polynices into exile. Eteocles becomes the king of Thebes and Polynices goes off to Argos where he marries Argeia. Polynices next persuades his father-in-law to wage war on Thebes, at which time Polynices and six other warriors join forces to make up the Seven against Thebes. Eteocles and Polynices meet in single combat and slew each other while Creon, their mother's brother, becomes the king of Thebes, ordering that Eteocles, the defender of the city, be buried with full honors, but refusing to bury Polynices, thus denying him peace in the Underworld. Nevertheless, the definitive account of Oedipus is Sophocles' *Oedipus Rex*.

The opening scene takes place in Thebes, before the palace gates. The daughters of Oedipus, Antigone and Ismene, discuss Creon's edict that Eteocles will be buried "with lawful rights" in the earth, "to have his honor among the dead," but that Polynices must lie unburied, "a dainty treasure for the birds that see him, for their feast's delight." Antigone declares that she will not obey Creon's decree, despite all of Ismene's remonstrations to the contrary. "Be as you choose to be; but for myself / I myself will bury him. It will be good / to die, so doing." A noble and courageous young woman, Antigone is devoted not only to the memory of her brother and her responsibilities to her family but to her own unswerving principles, to the laws of the gods as opposed to the laws of man. Ismene, a gentle and passive girl, accepts the rule of Creon; and therefore cannot defy the law of the state. "[T]o act in defiance of the citizenry / my nature does not give me means for that." Antigone offers a harsh rebuke, telling Ismene that she alone will bury their brother. As the two sisters leave, the Chorus of Theban Elders enters and sings an ode about the attack of the Seven against Thebes, of Polynices' murderous betrayal of his city and the fatal combat between two brothers. "Only those two wretches born of one father and mother . . . worked out their share in a common death."

Creon enters with two attendants. He speaks of his decree concerning the burial of the two brothers, which elicits a very lukewarm response from the Leader of the Chorus. A Sentry then enters and reports, in a frightened and rather clumsy manner, that someone has mysteriously removed Polynices' corpse. The Leader of the Chorus suggests that this may be the work of the gods, but this idea only makes Creon angry. "Stop, before your words fill even me with rage, / that you should be exposed as a fool, and you so old." Creon dismisses the Sentry, threatening him and his associates with torture and death if they do not find the person responsible for removing the body. "You will hang alive till you open up this outrage."

When Creon and the Guard leave the stage, the Chorus sings a beautiful ode on man, the greatest marvel of all the marvels on earth. "He it is again who wears away / the Earth, oldest of gods, immortal, unwearied, / as the plow winds across her from year to year." Yet, though he has the powers of thought and speech, and despite all his achievements, man is still the victim of death. When he honors the gods and upholds the laws of the land, his state flourishes, but the corrupt man has no nation. "No city / has he with whom dwells dishonor / prompted by recklessness."

The Sentry then returns with Antigone, calling out for Creon and declaring he has found her burying her Polynices. Creon questions her, and Antigone unflinchingly defends her disobedience of Creon's edict, saying that in burying her brother she was obeying the laws of the gods. "God's ordinances, unwritten and secure. / They are not of today and yesterday; / they live forever; none knows when first they were." Ismene next enters and offers to share Antigone's punishment, bravely telling her sister that "in your troubles I am not ashamed / to sail with you the sea of suffering," but Antigone refuses, saying that Ismene had previously chosen life. Ismene asks Creon if he really intends to carry out his threat and kill Antigone, who is betrothed to his own son, Haemon. Creon's responds that Antigone must die. "Death—it is death that will stop the marriage for me." Ismene and Antigone leave the stage, guarded by attendants.

The Chorus sings an ode in which it relates the present suffering of Antigone to the history of sorrow of the family of Labdacus, father of Laius. "I see the ancient evils of Labdacus' house / are heaped on the evils of the dead. / No generation frees another, some god / strikes them down; there is no deliverance." It should be noted that the theme of conflict and suffering continuing through the generations from parent to child is a familiar one in Greek myth and tragedy.

When Haemon next enters, he tries to persuade his father to change his mind about Antigone's punishment, declaring that her deed was glorious and that the citizens of the city mourn with her, while observing that Creon is viewed as a tyrant. "Your face is terrible to a simple citizen / it frightens him from words you dislike to hear. / But what I can hear, in the dark, are things like these: / the city mourns for this girl; they think she is dying / . . . for the most glorious acts." When he realizes that Creon cannot be moved, Haemon calls him unjust, "[y]ou would be a fine dictator of a desert," and as he leaves, he tells his father that he will never see him again. Creon informs the Chorus that he intends to imprison Antigone in a rocky vault, where she can pray to Hades for release.

Antigone comes out of the palace, to be lead to her death by Creon's attendants. In a lyrical dialogue with the Chorus, Antigone tragically observes that she will never see the sunlight again, never participate in the traditional marriage rites, but instead will be married to Hades. "I am alive but Hades who gives sleep to everyone / is leading me to the shores of Acheron . . . My husband is to be the Lord of Death." Creon enters and dispassionately urges the attendants to imprison Antigone in the vault and leave her. This is Creon's way of avoiding a direct murder of Antigone; as he says, his hands are clean, yet he knows she will die in the vault. "[W]e are guiltless in respect of her, this girl. But living above, among the rest of us, this life / she shall certainly lose."

After Antigone has been taken away, a boy leads in the blind prophet, Tiresias. Tiresias rebukes Creon for allowing the body of Polynices to lie unburied and for sending Antigone to her death. "This is the city's sickness—and your plans are the cause of it. / For our altars and our sacrificial hearths / are filled with the carrion meat of birds and dogs, / torn from the flesh of Oedipus' poor son. / So the gods will not take our prayers or sacrifice." Tiresias predicts that Creon will regret his tyrannical acts. "And you must realize / that you will not outlive many cycles more . . . for you have thrust one that belongs above / below the earth, and bitterly dishonoured / a living soul by lodging her in the grave." Once he leaves his arrogant posture and finally takes Tiresias' sage advice seriously, Creon becomes deeply disturbed. As he finally accepts the advice of the Leader of the Chorus to free Antigone from her tomb, he and his servants rush off to the vault.

A Messenger then appears to relate the dreadful tale about the deaths of Antigone and Haemon. Eurydice, the wife of Creon, enters and asks the Messenger to tell her the whole story. He tells of how Creon and his servants entered the tomb to find that Antigone had hanged herself, while Haemon, embracing her dead body, wept over his bride and his father's evil deeds. When the young man saw Creon, he spat in his father's face, then drew his sword and, as Creon fled, killed himself. "[T]he poor wretch in anger at himself / leaned on his sword and drove it halfway in, / into his ribs. Then he folded the girl to him . . . So he has won / the pitiful fulfillment of his marriage / within death's house." After hearing this terrible report Eurydice enters the palace. The Messenger follows shortly after. Then Creon enters with attendants carrying the body of Haemon. Soon the Messenger appears again to announce that Eurydice has killed herself. "She died, poor lady, by recent violence upon herself." The doors of the palace are opened and her corpse is revealed. Creon accepts his guilt for the death of his loved ones. As he laments over the bodies of his wife and his son, he calls himself their slayer, declaring that he is "no more a live man than one dead." ❀

List of Characters in
Antigone

Antigone, daughter of Oedipus and Jocasta, gives her brother Polynices a proper burial against the edict of Creon. She courageously accepts the punishment of death, knowing that she has done right by her family and the gods.

Ismene is the gentle and quiet sister of Antigone who obeys the edict of Creon and refuses to help Antigone bury Polynices. When Antigone is sentenced to death, Ismene offers to die with her but Antigone rejects the offer, saying that she chose life before in obeying Creon.

The **Chorus of Theban Elders** reacts to events happening onstage and provides the background mood. It provides a guide for how the audience is supposed to interpret, or how not to interpret the play.

Creon, Antigone's uncle and the new king of Thebes, declares that Polynices should not have a proper burial and prohibits his family from giving him one. When he discovers that Antigone has broken this rule, he refuses to relent and sentences her to death. He changes his mind after being rebuked by Tiresias, the blind prophet, but it is too late. His stubbornness results in the destruction of Antigone, his son and wife, and ultimately himself.

Haemon, son of Creon, is engaged to marry Antigone. He pleads for his father to spare Antigone's life but to no avail. He ultimately kills himself when he discovers Antigone has committed suicide.

Tiresias, the blind prophet, advises Creon to spare Antigone or he will bring disaster upon Thebes.

Eurydice is the wife of Creon who commits suicide when she discovers that both her son Haemon and Antigone are dead.

Polynices is the son of Oedipus and brother of Antigone who battles his brother for the throne of Thebes and is subsequently killed by his brother Eteocles. Antigone buries his body against the edict of Creon.

Eteocles is the youngest son of Oedipus and brother of Antigone who battles with his brother for the throne of Thebes. He is killed by Polynices and given a proper burial by Creon. ❀

Critical Views on
Antigone

A. T. Von S. Bradshaw on the Watchmen

[A. T. Von S. Bradshaw is the author of "The Watchman Scenes in the *Antigone* (1962). In the excerpt below from that article, Bradshaw discusses some questions in the critical debate regarding the time of day in which Antigone buried Polynices and the responsibilities of the watchmen.]

⟨. . .⟩ When is Antigone supposed to have buried the body, and what duties have the watchmen been carrying out? ⟨. . .⟩

A more recent critic, Professor H.D.F. Kitto, in his *Form and Meaning in Drama,* p. 155, offers an explanation similar to Jebb's except for one important detail: 'When they [the watchmen] came to their post it was of course night-time, and there was nothing whatever to arouse their suspicions—no cart-tracks, no up-cast of earth. All seemed as it should be. Then dawn came, and the watch saw that all was not as it should be: the body was covered with light dust.' But the 'post' to which the watchmen come can only be the body of Polyneices. Can we suppose that the men began their watch over a body which they could identify on the corpse-strewn battlefield as that of Polyneices, but which at the same time was so effectively covered with earth that, when viewed in the clear light of day, it could be said to have disappeared. Yet in the one detail which makes nonsense of this explanation and also distinguishes it from Jebb's, Kitto is certainly right, though he takes no pains to emphasize the point. In saying that it was night-time when the watchmen came to their post he implies that Antigone must have done her deed in the night-time and also of course that the first scene, in which she disclosed her intentions to Ismene, took place in the night-time. That the play begins in the night is an important fact. As the fact itself has been missed or ignored by a large number of critics, it will be necessary to demonstrate it as well as to bring out its importance. ⟨. . .⟩

As it is clearly absurd to imagine the night-watch mounting guard over the corpse after Antigone has covered it with earth, it follows that she must be understood to have performed the burial while the night watchmen were on duty. Once this is realized, the problems listed as (1), (2), and (4) are immediately seen to be resolved. The Watchman has the best of reasons for being afraid for his life: he has failed in his duty. No wonder he emphasizes the fact that no pickaxe, spade, or waggon has been used: if they had, the complicity of the watchmen could not be denied. Creon's anger is not evidence of a tyrant's irrational fury: he has good cause to believe that his own men have betrayed him. It is remarkable that T. von Wilamowitz, who, unlike most English critics, understood that the watchmen are supposed to be on guard while Antigone carries out her task, completely missed the point of 249–52. He suggested that, as it must be a laborious business to cover a body with earth by hand, the Watchman might reasonably expect tools to have been used; as they were not, he naturally remarks on the fact to give Creon and the audience some idea of the manner of Polyneices' burial (op. cit., p. 27). This is trivial. It is perfectly plain that the Watchman is doing precisely what his previous behaviour should lead us to expect him to do: he is primarily concerned to avoid blame, and he therefore begins his story by stressing that this was no ordinary burial involving tools and a cart and the breaking of ground, which no guards could have honestly failed to detect. Wilamowitz manufactured a new problem at this point: from the description of the ground in 250–3 he concludes that the surface must have been entirely bare and asks where Antigone got the dust with which she covered the corpse. W. Schmid (Schmid–Stählin, *Gr. Lit.* I. ii. 349, n. 3) was impressed by this difficulty. But ⟨*styflos*⟩ and ⟨*chersos*⟩ surely have a simple significance, simpler indeed than Jebb's interpretation; for Jebb thought that the adjectives indicate why no footprints are traceable (248 n.). Campbell's explanation— 'undisturbed by implements of husbandry'—is perhaps nearer the truth. But this is a matter of grave-digging, not husbandry.

—A. T. Von S. Bradshaw, "The Watchman Scenes in the *Antigone*." *The Classical Quarterly* vol. XII, no. 2 (1962): pp. 201–2.

MICHAEL EWANS ON THE LITERARY ORIGINS OF *ANTIGONE*

[Michael Ewans is the translator and commentator of *Georg Buchner's* Woyzek (1989) and the author of *Wagner and Aeschylus:* The Ring *and the* Oresteia (1983). In the excerpt below from his introduction to *Four Dramas of Maturity,* Ewans discusses the literary origins of the story of *Antigone* and its heroine.]

Few debates are as sterile as the academic discussions that were once devoted to the question whether Antigone or Kreon is the central figure in this drama. *Antigone,* like *Young Women of Trachis,* provides a powerful reminder that the Greeks viewed individual tragedy not in isolation, but in the context of its impact on the *oikos* and the *polis*. In performance, without the benefit of hindsight leafing through the text in the study, the drama is neither Antigone's tragedy nor Kreon's. It simply unfolds, with one or other of the two characters predominant at different times.

Antigone commands the playing space in the three scenes in which she appears; but by the end Kreon is the central character: the final image is his exit broken by the loss, in one day, by his own folly, of both son and wife. Antigone deserves the title role because her courage and conviction, her absolute and self-sacrificing defiance of Kreon's edict is the catalyst that creates the whole tragedy; but as the drama unfolds in performance, Kreon's incapacity to handle the political and familial situation that he has created becomes more and more central.

The attempt to place Antigone at the centre is partly the result of a long tradition of male worship of the martyred, virginal heroine; but it also grows, more justifiably, from a feeling that her absolute stance is morally right, and a reluctance to allow Kreon to dominate because he is not an acceptable 'tragic hero'—if Aristotle was right, when he declared that true tragedy is not to be found in the spectacle of a wicked or stupid man encountering his deserts.

Kreon in his final agonies has none of the nobility of Oidipous in the Finale to *Oidipous the King,* and he ignores his Councillors' repeated admonitions that silence, rather than self-indulgent lamentation, is the proper response to the deaths of his son and wife. Nobility in a female character who goes to her death long before the end, followed by ignoble agony in an unworthy man who holds the focus to the end, have severely puzzled many (predominantly male) literary critics; and they have headed in three equally misguided directions. Some classical scholars have picked away at Antigone's nobility, trying to see her as just too extreme and single-minded; others have attempted to make Kreon into an archetype of true statecraft tragically subverted by events; a third group diagnoses flaws in them both. Only a few critics have had the courage to argue for the only reading that responds to the text in performance. As the drama unfolds, it becomes clear that Kreon is a paranoid autocrat, and Antigone was right to transgress against the role expected of a woman in fifth century Athens, and bury her brother herself.

—Michael Ewans, ed., *Four Dramas of Maturity: Aias, Antigone, Young Women of Trachis, Oidipous the King.* London: Everyman (1999): pp. xlviii–xlix.

ROBERT GOHEEN ON RECURRING IMAGERY

[Robert F. Goheen is the author of *The Human Nature of a University* (1969). In the excerpt below from the Introduction to his book, Goheen discusses some aspects of the recurrence of imagery in *Antigone*.]

The Fact of Recurrence

Recurrence of imagery is a fact of the *Antigone* which we have already stated to be one of the keys to the total structure, and it is a fact with which we shall be concerned for most of the rest of this essay. It is of significance for us in several ways and on several levels.

At a rather elementary level it serves as an indication that an unobtrusive image or one which might otherwise be regarded as "dead" is in fact alive within a pattern of meanings created by the poet about it. Consider, for example, the military terms in the opening speech of the play:

> And now what is this new thing which they say that the
> general (*stratêgon*) has just had heralded to the city and all
> its people: Do you know? Have you heard? Or do you fail
> to see that the evils of your enemies are marching (*stei-*
> *chonta*) on your friends?

When Antigone refers to Creon here as the *stratêgos* (a general term
for the leader of the state in many tragedies, a military general, a
chief executive in the Athenian state) the term may seem only general and of not much particular significance at first. At the same
time, the implication of military rigor to be felt in the term is given
support by the military implication of the other word, *steichonta*,
which follows closely behind. This later term often means only to
proceed, but it is connected closely with marching and military
columns. Together these two images in the overtones of Antigone's
first reference to Creon have connection to, and show their vitality in
their bearing upon, Creon's second and crucial statement of political
principle, which, as we shall see more fully, rests upon a military
conception and includes obedience "to small orders and just orders
and orders of the opposite kind." And here, as Antigone's initial,
latent characterization of Creon's manner of rule foresees, well in
advance of the vision of the other characters, the limited character of
that rule and expresses it in just the terms which Creon later brings
into the open, the recurrences of military imagery take us to a further level of meaning and a more internal kind of awareness—that
of Antigone's intuitive knowledge and its validity, despite the general
discredit which it suffers for over half of the play.

Another example is worth noticing, for it involves an almost
hoary metaphor being called to life and being so developed as to
take us into the clash of points of view on one of the central issues of
the play. This is the sequence built on *hyperbainein* (to overstep,
transgress) in application to law and religious principles. The first
appearance is 449. Creon asks Antigone,

> Did you then dare to overstep these laws?

She replies affirmatively and in her famous speech of defense presents the righteousness of her conduct as against his view that he, a
mortal, could override (*hyperdramein*) the unwritten and imperish-
able laws of the gods. Creon returns to his original expression in

481, and the momentary balance and clash of these images subsides for the time being. But following this scene, the Chorus recalls Creon's original term to generalize upon Zeus's invincible power and law of retribution against human *transgression*. As a result of the previous exchange with this image in relation to human and divine law, suggestive overtones are aroused when the Chorus continues and applies this general theme with a further pedal image:

> For far-ranging expectation is to many men a comfort but to many the deceit which follows light desire. Disillusionment comes to him who knows not until he burn his foot in the hot fire.

—Robert F. Goheen, *The Imagery of Sophocles'* Antigone: *A Study of Poetic Language and Structure*. Princeton, New Jersey: Princeton University Press (1951): pp. 9–11.

G. M. KIRKWOOD ON THE CONTRAST BETWEEN ANTIGONE AND CREON

[G. M. Kirkwood is the editor of *Selections from Pindar* (1982) and *Poetry and Poetics from Ancient Greece to the Renaissance* (1975). In the excerpt below from the chapter entitled "Character Portrayal," Kirkwood discusses the complexity of the contrast between Antigone and Creon.]

That a contrast between Antigone and Creon lies at the heart of the drama can be taken for granted. Our task in this section will be to examine two matters: the complexity of this contrast, and the subsidiary character relationships and their effect on the action. We shall review first the secondary contrasts and end with the main clash between Antigone and Creon.

Antigone and Ismene are together in two scenes, in the prologue and at the end of the second episode. The contrast between them is not that of devotion to a cause *vs.* timidity; it is more complex than that and more revealing of the character of Antigone. Of course Antigone is devoted and has a cause; and Ismene, by contrast, is timid. But to what, exactly, is Antigone's devotion, and what does it indicate about her? The contrast with Ismene helps us to answer these questions. In the prologue Antigone's first concern is not for religious duty, which looms so large in her scene with Creon. Her first reaction is a personal one; the matter is one of family loyalty, where, she feels, Creon has no right to intrude. Antigone is intense, as we see from the opening line on; her greeting to Ismene has more of intimacy and passion than of loving gentleness. To Creon's clumsy interference with her duty to her family, she responds with instinctive hostility. She is furious that Creon should seek to legislate to her in a matter so personal to her: "Such conditions they say the worthy Creon has proclaimed for you and me—yes, even for me" (32–33)! The burial of Polyneices becomes for her the very touchstone of nobility, and she declares that Ismene by her attitude toward it will show "Whether you are of noble nature ⟨. . .⟩ or base though your parents were good" (38). Like Ajax and Deianeira, Antigone has an unhesitating devotion to her concept of what is becoming to the ⟨noble⟩.

In all this there is no thought of the ⟨agrapta nomima⟩; up to this point Antigone has not reflected and has not formulated her instinctive idealism. She is not to be thought of as primarily a philosopher or an embodiment of the reasoned way of life. By the contrasting reaction of Ismene we understand more clearly what Antigone is. Ismene's conduct is equally instinctive. Suddenly confronted with a bold and illegal scheme, she shrinks at once, for her instinct is to obey, just as surely as Antigone's is to exercise her own will: she is a woman, and cannot fight against men (61–62); she must obey (47, 59, 79); Antigone's plan lacks common sense (68); those below will forgive her for not acting (65–66); she cannot act ⟨via politon⟩ (79). So far as moral attitude is concerned, there is no fundamental difference; Ismene is as aware as Antigone of the wrongness of Creon's edict. The difference is in personality: Ismene is without the imperiousness, willfulness, and single-mindedness of her sister; she is prudent and sees other aspects of the situation. Antigone has eyes for only the one issue that is to her all-important.

There is another contrast between them. When Ismene shows reluctance to act, Antigone becomes instantly hostile. She declares bitterly that she would not now accept her sister's help if it were offered (69–70); when Ismene advises silence and says that she too will be silent about the plan to bury Polyneices, Antigone angrily bids her tell it to all (84–87). Antigone promises Ismene the hatred of their dead brother and of herself (93–94); Ismene in the last words of the prologue assures Antigone of her love, mad though she may be.

—G. M. Kirkwood, *A Study of Sophoclean Drama*. Ithaca, New York: Cornell University Press (1958): pp. 118–20.

Marsh McCall on the Two Burials in *Antigone*

[Marsh McCall is the author of *Ancient Rhetorical Theories of Simile and Comparison* (1969) and the editor of *Aeschylus: A Collection of Critical Essays* (1972). In the excerpt below from his article, "Divine and human action in Sophocles: the two burials of the *Antigone*," McCall sets forth the questions posed in the critical debate concerning the burial of Polynices.]

Sir Richard Jebb called attention long ago to a problem of motivation in Antigone's presumed double burial of Polynices, and he remarked, 'I have never seen this question put or answered'. Were he alive, he might well wish he had never raised the question, so frequent and various have been the answers proposed during the intervening three-quarters of a century. It has even been suggested that concern for the question is irrelevant to the text or fostered merely to produce 'original' literary criticism. The number of able scholars who have dealt with the problem of the double burial, however, would appear to reflect a real uneasiness about the true meaning of the text. ⟨. . .⟩

If Antigone alone performed both burials, then Sophocles felt that two burials supply something to the development of the play which a single burial would not. It has never been argued persuasively that the second burial is required for religious purposes. The guard explicitly credits the first burial with all necessary observances. The purpose of the second burial must be dramatic. More 'dramatic' solutions for Antigone's return to her brother have been proposed than can be noted here. For the most part, however, they may be grouped under the following headings. (1) Antigone's return signifies her ⟨*hamartia*⟩, the stubbornness which forms her tragic flaw.

(2) Antigone in some way *wants* to be caught. (3) The Athenian audience does not really notice, or at least does not question, the two visits. (4) It is simply a natural and dutiful act of devotion for Antigone to return to her brother, especially on learning that he has been uncovered. (5) Two burials increase the suspense of the play and serve to show Antigone triumphant before we see her defeated and captured. Clearly these categories impinge upon one another, and writers have not always restricted themselves to one alone. ⟨. . .⟩

Two other questions may also be asked. If the second burial is only a dramatic device, why does its character seem so different from the first burial? There, Antigone accomplishes her mission with stealth; the guards are wholly unaware of her presence. At the second burial, on the other hand, once the dust storm has lifted, Antigone is perceived making no effort either to hide herself or to keep silent. She conducts the first burial with caution, the second with abandon. Her approach to the second burial might be used to support the theory that she desires capture, but then why does she wait until a second burial to expose herself? The difference in the *modus operandi* of the two burials must be taken as a dramatic inconsistency in any theory involving Antigone's performance of both of them, unless we say that she was required religiously to return and lament over the body, and by so doing reveals herself. This has been argued but, like other solutions of a religious nature, without compelling evidence.

Secondly, why does Antigone make no mention of the double act of devotion to her brother in the scenes from her capture to her final exit? One would think that in her defiance of Creon and in the maintenance of the higher justice of her actions such a mention would find natural and emphatic expression. Yet it never occurs. At 442, when Creon first addresses Antigone after the guard's reluctant indictment of her, *he* uses a generalizing plural, ⟨*tade*⟩, to refer to her actions (he of course is quick to attribute both burials to her), and she assents to his words, but he seems to be thinking mainly of the second burial, and in any case ⟨*tade*⟩ can signify singular as easily as plural. At 542, Antigone rebuffs her sister with a reference in the singular to what she has done.

—Marsh McCall, "Divine and Human Action in Sophocles: The Two Burials of the *Antigone.*" *Yale Classical Studies,* vol. XXII (1972): pp. 103–7.

[Edouard Schuré is the author of *Evolution divine* (1912) and *Femmes inspiratrices et poetes annonciateurs* (1925). In the excerpt below from Chapter V, "The Mystery of Eleusis," Schuré discusses *Antigone* in terms of the psychological evolution of the heroine.]

The 'Antigone', Revealer of the Eternal-Feminine and of Universal Love

We may now attempt to pierce the secret of the tragedy of *Antigone*, the conclusion of the great Theban trilogy.

This drama represents the blossoming of the thought of Sophokles. It brings before us the most extraordinary psychological evolution that has ever been represented on the stage. This evolution not only comes about in the heroine, it spreads all around and affects the whole city. Let us follow the stages of this metamorphosis which seems miraculous, though the magic of art makes it inevitable.

The city of Thebes is emerging from the horrors of a civil war which has grafted itself upon the disasters of the family of Oedipus. The sons of the incestuous king have provoked this war in an attempt to usurp the reins of government. The besiegers have been repulsed, but the two rival brothers have inflicted deadly blows each upon the other. Thebes is freed from her external enemies, though as completely crushed by her misfortunes as if she had been vanquished. Only apparently now does she believe in her Gods, in divine justice. Two powers alone rule over men's hearts and cause them to bow their head: Hatred and Fear. Kreon, an ambitious upstart, a clever and intriguing tyrant, crafty and obstinate, has attained to power. No longer having another master, the city of Thebes trembles before him. Straightway he intends to give the people a proof of his absolute authority. The body of Eteokles, the defender of Thebes, has been buried in accordance with the usual rites; but the body of Polyneikes, the enemy of his country, whose sole representative Kreon henceforth wished to be, is deprived of funeral honours, his body rots in the sunlight, a prey to dogs and vultures. And such is to be the lot of those who dare to disobey the tyrant of Thebes. We must remember that the Greeks believed the souls of the unburied dead to be condemned to endless wanderings, to eternal sufferings. Only one person, Antigone, in all the city dares to oppose the decree and confront the tyrant. What is it that gives such extraordinary courage to a defenceless virgin, of royal blood, true, though owing her birth to the crime of incest? ⟨. . .⟩

⟨. . .⟩ Day has not yet risen upon the sleeping city. In the semi-darkness of the approaching dawn, Antigone and Ismene, the two daughters of Oedipus, stealthily leave the palace of Kreon. News of the sinister decree which condemns to the gibbet the body of Polyneikes, has reached them. For fear of eaves-dropping, they have left the palace to consult together. One trembles with indignation, the other with fear. The courageous elder sister informs the younger of her resolve to confront the tyrant, and, in spite of him, to bury the body of her brother. She asks Ismene to join her in the act. The timid and gentle Ismene, however, lacks her sister's fine courage. She shrinks from the project, alleging the folly and danger of such an act undertaken by two feeble women. Whereupon Antigone answers with cold disdain: 'I would neither urge thee nor, if thou wert still willing to act, wouldst thou do it pleasingly with me at least. But be thou of what sort it seems good to thee, I however will bury him. It is glorious for me to die, doing this. ⟨. . .⟩ From this moment, a wide gulf separates her from her sister. Subsequently, when the feeble though kind and faithful Ismene, moved by her sister's tragic fate, wishes to follow her in death, the latter proudly replies: 'No, thou hast chosen to live and I to die.'

—Edouard Schuré, *The Genesis of Tragedy and The Sacred Drama of Eleusis*, trans. Fred Rothwell. London: Rudolf Steiner Publish Co. and New York: Anthroposophic Press (1936): pp. 226–29.

DAVID SEALE ON THE REPRESENTATION OF ANTIGONE'S OPENING ADDRESS

[David Seale is the author of *Vision and Stagecraft in Sophocles* (1982). In the excerpt below from the chapter entitled "The *Antigone:* Concrete Visualisation," Seale discusses the dramatic representation of Antigone's elaborate opening address.]

O Ismene, my kindred sister, my own dearest sister . . .

The opening address is extraordinarily elaborate and signifies more than the conventional warmth of a family relationship; the keynote of the drama, kinship, is immediately sounded on the lips of her who is to stake her life on its obligations. This is Antigone, in her earliest youth. It is her secret initiative with her sister, Ismene, which sets the tragedy in motion. They stand before the royal palace at Thebes, the house that once belonged to their father. Family is indeed the subject-matter of the whole scene, the ill-starred family of Oedipus. We hear of the self-inflicted blindness of Oedipus himself, the suicide of his mother and wife, Jocasta, and now most recently, the mutual fratricide of his two sons, Eteocles and Polynices. His daughters, now before us, are the sole survivors (58). They are there together as a unit, in visual harmony, their closeness set against the verbal background of violent family conflict. And the question is whether they can overcome a new evil which has befallen them—*as a pair.*

The new evil of which Antigone speaks is the proclamation of Creon, now king, which prescribes discriminatory treatment for the bodies of her two brothers: Eteocles, the defender of the city, is to be buried with due honour; Polynices, who has invaded Thebes with foreign troops, is to be left unburied and unwept. The horror of the exposed corpse is impressed upon us by Antigone with shocking clarity; it will provide an unending feast for birds, as they see it from the air. But she intends to defy the proclamation and bury her brother's corpse at the risk of death by public stoning. Here, in the darkness of pre-dawn (16 and 100), Antigone tries to involve Ismene in her secret resolve. Her failure signals the breakup of this last family relationship and we watch the heroine of the tragedy come into being before our eyes. Ismene is cautious, obedient to male authority and lacks the courage of her convictions. Antigone is fearless, self-reliant and willing to die for hers. And she disdains Ismene's promise of concealment, ready to match Creon's 'proclamation' with her own, a love of kindred declared in deed (86–7). The growing rift which develops in the course of the scene culminates in their separate departures, a visible rupture of the initial harmony. The shape of the theatre makes this severance particularly impressive; Ismene withdraws unobtrusively to wait in the palace, Antigone leaves by a *parodos*. The independence, the single-mindedness, the open and solitary defiance are all there in the long walk from the scene. Antigone separates herself from all that Ismene is. And she abandons one who is no longer a sister, for she goes to be with the dead, the only kindred that remains to her. The exit of Antigone is an emblem of her absolute isolation.

For a moment the stage is empty. Then the Chorus enters from the other *parodos*, oblivious of the intrigue to which the audience has been privy and, as yet, unaware of Creon's proclamation. The personality of the Chorus is important. It consists of the elders of Thebes, who represent community. The conflict between private and public morality which lies at the heart of the tragedy is already foreshown in the scenic contrast, the desolate figure set against the harmonious group. As in the *Electra* the prologue is separated from the world of the play, and even more dramatically; Antigone is the main character and she is distinctive among the 'heroes' of Sophoclean tragedy in her given isolation from the Chorus, by age, by status and, uniquely, by sex. The elders have come to celebrate the city's glorious victory over the foreign invaders and they fill the scene with sound and movement as personal grief gives way to public exultation:

> Ray of the sun, fairest light that ever *appeared* [*phanen*]
> on seven-gated Thebe, you *appeared* [*ephanthēs*] finally,
> *eye* of golden day, having come above the streams of
> Dirce. . . . (100–5)

These first choral lyrics of the play, with one image of light piled upon another, echo and re-echo a visible joy. But the brilliant sunlight which they hail actually belongs to the previous day of victory and the dramatic sequence has it emerge from the pre-dawn darkness of Antigone's ominous venture. The ecstatic performance—and this is the land of Dionysus, the god of ecstasy (151–4)—is thus out of place, an illusion of brightness which has already passed, as the final image of night perhaps implies (152).

> —David Seale, *Vision and Stagecraft in Sophocles.* Chicago: Chicago University Press (1982): pp. 84–85.

[George Steiner is the author of *On Difficulty and Other Essays* (1978) and *Real Presences* (1989). In the excerpt below from Chapter II of his book, Steiner discusses the complexities of the Greek notion of invention as it applies to *Antigone*.]

Scholarly opinion today has it that the tragic tale of Antigone, as we know it, was most probably Sophocles' invention. In this context, it remains entirely unclear what is to be understood by 'invention'. Pausanias (ix. 25) mentions a piece of terrain outside Thebes, a furrow in the ground, which the local inhabitants ascribed to Antigone. This, they assured the traveller, was the indelible spoor left by Polyneices' corpse as Antigone dragged it to the funeral pyre. We have no way of telling whether this scenic marker precedes the literature or comes after it in illustration. It is supposed, with a fair measure of confidence, that the disasters of the clan of Laius and their effect on the early history of Thebes and of Argos were the subject of epic treatment as early as the second half of the eight century B.C. But nothing save small fragments of an *Oidipodeia* or *Thebais* has come down to us. A recently published and much-discussed papyrus assigns to Jocasta a commanding role in the Eteocles–Polyneices quarrel, but gives to this fratricidal affair a judicial and dynastic framework which differs markedly from Sophocles' (Polyneices has renounced his claims to alternating kingship in Thebes in exchange for the wealth, the treasures of the ⟨oikos⟩, bequeathed by Oedipus). It has been suggested that we have here an epic fragment or 'dramatic lyric' by Stesichorus, which would take us back to the late seventh or early sixth century. The obscurities in the arrangement of rotating kingship implicit in Sophocles' handling of the Eteocles–Polyneices conflict, the vestigial ambiguities in Creon's claim to legitimacy in Thebes, have led certain classical scholars and anthropologists to argue that the entire saga of Oedipus and his children mirrors a violent, obscure transition from a native matrilineal system to the patrilineal conventions of dynastic succession and property-division brought by the Dorian invaders. Far echoes of this crisis would emerge in Euripides' *Phoenician Women*, notably in lines 1586–8.

The survival of Oedipus and Jocasta into old age, as shown in Euripides' drama, Homer's famous allusion in the Iliad, iv. 394, to a son of Haemon, Pindar's reference, in his Second Olympian, to Polyneices' male heir, the Euripidean *Antigone,* and a disputed passage in a commentary by the Byzantine scholiast Aristophanes, demonstrate that Sophocles' version was not, or not at the outset, the only available or accepted one. This points either to variants in the legendary material or to liberties of invention taken by individual poets. The latter may have been greater than neo-classical and even nineteenth-century critics supposed. Knowing nothing about the part which Antigone may or may not have played in such epic texts as the *Thebais,* the *Oidipodeia,* the *Epigonoi,* the *Amphiarai Exelasis,* we can make no sensible guess as to relations between the extant myths and our play. What is, on present evidence, quite plausible is the hypothesis that Antigone's defiance of Creon's edict on the very night after the murderous battle, and the tragic collision provoked by this defiance, were Sophocles' 'idea'. The representation of this theme at the close of Aeschylus' *Seven Against Thebes,* with its strong hints of a fortunate resolution, is now thought, though not unanimously, to be a post-Sophoclean addition to an earlier play. It would signal the success and fascination of Sophocles' invention.

> —George Steiner, *Antigones.* New York and Oxford: Oxford University Press (1984): pp. 110–12.

⊗

R. P. WINNINGTON-INGRAM ON HUMAN AND DIVINE AGENCY

[R. P. Winnington-Ingram is the author of *Studies in Aeschylus* (1983) and *Fragments of Unknown Greek Texts with Musical Notation* (1955). In the excerpt below from the chapter entitled "Fate in Sophocles," Winnington-Ingram discusses the role of human and divine agency for the heroine, Antigone.]

We shall all die, at a moment unknown and in circumstances no one can foresee: this is the ultimate dispensation. The Greeks, at some early stage in their thinking about the world, came to conceive of powers which they called Moirai. If these were spirits who presided over birth as well as determining death, it is not hard to see why. The individual comes to birth with an apportionment (a *moira*) of life, and nothing is more striking in the lot of human beings than the difference in their life-spans and the unpredictability of their deaths. There must be some power or powers which determine these things: not only birth and death but the events of life, particularly perhaps those which are dramatic and disastrous and lead towards death. ⟨. . .⟩

If the Greeks spoke of a *moira* in connection with an individual's lot, they also spoke of his *daimon*. This word (which may or may not mean 'apportioner') has a stronger suggestion of personal agency but is conceived in this association vaguely, as a divine power co-existent with a man and determining the course of his life: when it determines for good, he is *eudaimon*, but *dusdaimon* when it determines for ill. ⟨. . .⟩

Divine power broods over the action. Ask the question Why?, and there is always a divine component, though not necessarily the sole component, in the answer. When we ask the same question of *Oedipus Tyrannus*, what shall we find? Or of *Antigone*?

Why did these events fall out as they did? Why for Antigone? Why for Creon? To the latter question there might seem a simple answer in the closing anapaests: he is punished for his arrogance and impiety. ⟨. . .⟩

Antigone is more important—Antigone and her fate. The word *moira* does not occur in the closing scene (though *potmos* does): indeed it occurs only twice in the play, but once in an interesting context, where it is associated with the adjective *moiridia*. This is in the Fourth Stasimon. Antigone has left the stage for a living tomb, and the Chorus call to mind other figures of legend whose fates were in some way similar. The figures who stand closest to her are Danae, in the first stanza, and Cleopatra, in the fourth—both women, both innocent victims. In the first case we hear of the terrible power of fate (951f.); in the second we are told how the long-lived Moirai bore upon Cleopatra also—on Cleopatra as well as upon the child Antigone. The Chorus are confronted with a ghastly event for which they find it hard to account (they have tried out their theology in the *kommos*): the notion of fate comes into their minds.

Indeed Antigone has already sung of her *daimon* (833) and her *potmos* (881), but also of the *potmos* which she shares with the whole ill-famed family of the Labdacids (857ff.). If the antecedents of Creon are dramatically unimportant, it is otherwise with the heroine; and this is not only because she has inherited from her father that 'harshness' and 'self-willed temper' which enabled her to do what she did. She acts and suffers as a member of a doomed family. This is brought out in the Prologos, in the opening speech of Antigone and Ismene's recital (49–57) of the terrible events they both have known. And if, as is understandable, for them the horror begins with Oedipus and they speak only of the small immediate group of *philoi* that constituted their world, Creon takes matters back to Laius whose reign was within his experience and that of the Chorus. The doom of the Labdacids is the theme of the Second Stasimon. The ode comes near the half-way mark of the play: it is long and elaborate and, in much of its language and thought, highly traditional if not Aeschylean. The name of Zeus is central to it—the Zeus that Antigone saw (2f.) as accomplishing evils upon her and Ismene, the Zeus from whom she will claim an authority for her act of rebellion. Close to Zeus come the nether gods and an Erinys. The ode begins with *ate* and ends with *ate*. For the theological interpretation of events it is likely to have crucial importance.

—R. P. Winnington-Ingram, *Sophocles: An Interpretation*. Cambridge, London and New York: Cambridge University Press (1980): pp. 150–51, 164–66.

Works by Sophocles

Ajax, ca. 447 B.C.

Antigone, ca. 442 B.C.

Ichneutai, ca. 440 B.C. (the satyr play).

Oedipus the King, ca. 430 B.C.

Electra, ca. 418–414 B.C.

The Women of Trachis, ca. 413 B.C.

Philoctetes, 409 B.C.

Oedipus at Colonus, produced in 401 B.C. after Sophocles' death.

Works About
Sophocles

Ahl, Frederick. *Sophocles' Oedipus: Evidence and Self-Conviction.* Ithaca: Cornell University Press, 1991.

Belfiore, Elizabeth S. *Murder Among Friends: Violation of Philia in Greek Tragedy.* New York: Oxford University Press, 2000.

Benardete, Seth. *Sacred Transgressions: A Reading of Sophocles'* Antigone. Indiana: St. Augustine's Press, 1999.

———. *The Argument of the Action: Essays on Greek Poetry and Philosophy.* Chicago: University of Chicago Press, 2000.

Boegehold, Alan L. *When a Gesture Was Expected: A Selection of Examples from Archaic and Classical Greek Literature.* New Jersey: Princeton University Press, 1999.

Budelmann, Felix. *The Language of Sophocles: Communality, Communication, and Involvement.* New York: Cambridge University Press, 2000.

Burkert, Walter. *Oedipus, Oracles, and Meaning: From Sophocles to Umberto Eco.* Toronto: The University of Toronto, 1991.

Burnett, Anne Pippin. *Revenge in Attic and Later Tragedy.* California: University of California Press, 1998.

Burton, R. W. B. *The Chorus in Sophocles' Tragedies.* Oxford: Clarendon Press; New York: Oxford University Press, 1980.

Bushnell, Rebecca W. *Prophesying Tragedy: Sign and Voice in Sophocles' Theban Plays.* Ithaca, New York: Cornell University Press, 1988.

Butler, Judith. *Antigone's Claim: Kinship Between Life and Death.* New York: Columbia University Press, 2000.

Buxton, R. G. A. *Sophocles.* Oxford: Clarendon Press; New York: Oxford University Press, 1984.

Daniels, Charles B., and Sam Scully. *What Really Goes on in Sophocles' Theban Plays.* Maryland: University Press of America, 1996.

Davis, Michael. *Ancient Tragedy and the Origins of Modern Science.* Carbondale: Southern Illinois University Press, 1988.

Dawe, Roger David. *Sophocles: The Classical Heritage.* New York: Garland Publishers, 1996.

Ditmars, Elizabeth Van Nes. *Sophocles' Antigone, Lyric Shape and Meaning.* Pisa: Giardini, 1992.

Edmunds, Lowell. *Theatrical Space and Historical Place in Sophocles' Oedipus at Colonus.* Maryland: Rowman & Littlefield Publishers, 1996.

Fergusson, Francis. *McCormick, John; Core, George. Sallies of the Mind.* New Jersey: Transaction, 1998.

Foley, Helene P. *Female Acts in Greek Tragedy.* New Jersey: Princeton University Press, 2001.

Gardiner, Cynthia P. *The Sophoclean Chorus: A Study of Character and Function.* Iowa City: University of Iowa Press, 1987.

Goward, Barbara. *Telling Tragedy: Narrative Technique in Aeschylus, Sophocles and Euripides.* London: Duckworth, 1999.

Griffith, R. Drew. *The Theatre of Apollo: Divine Justice and Sophocles' Oepidus the King.* Montreal: McGill-Queen University Press, 1996.

Handley, Eric. *Stage Directions: Essays in Ancient Drama in Honor of E. W. Handley.* London: Institute of Classical Studies, University of London School of Advanced Study, 1995.

Hogan, James C. *A Commentary on the Plays of Sophocles.* Carbondale: Southern Illinois University Press, 1991.

Knox, Bernard, and Mac Gregor Walker. *Oepidus at Thebes: Sophocles' Tragic Hero and His Time.* New Haven: Yale University Press, 1998.

Lloyd-Jones, Hugh, and Nigel G. Wilson. *Sophocles: Second Thoughts.* Gottingen: Vandenhoeck and Ruprecht, 1997.

Lloyd-Jones, Hugh and Jasper Griffin. *Sophocles Revisited: Essays presented to Sir Hugh Lloyd-Jones.* London: New York: Oxford University Press, 1999.

Mallard, William. *The Reflection of Theology in Literature: A Case Study in Theology and Culture.* San Antonio: Trinity University Press, 1977.

Minadeo, Richard. *The Thematic Sophocles.* Amsterdam: A. M. Hakkert, 1994.

Nagele, Rainer. *Echoes of Translation: Reading Between Texts.* Baltimore: Johns Hopkins University Press, 1997.

Neary, John. *Like and Unlike God: Religious Imaginations in Modern and Contemporary Fiction.* Georgia: Scholars Press, 1999.

Nortwick, Thomas Van. *Oedipus: The Meaning of a Masculine Life.* Norman: University of Oklahoma Press, 1998.

Ormand, Kirk. *Exchange and the Maiden: Marriage in Sophoclean Tragedy.* Austin: University of Texas Press, 1999.

Oudemans, Th. C. W., and A. P. M. H. Lardinois. *Tragic Ambiguity: Anthropology, Philosophy and Sophocles'* Antigone. Leiden and New York: E. J. Brill, 1987.

Padilla, Mark William. *Rites of Passage in Ancient Greece: Literature, Religion, Society.* Pennsylvania: Bucknell University Press; London: Associated University Presses, 1999.

Peradotto, John; Falkner, Thomas M.; Felson, Nancy; Konstan, David. *Contextualizing Classics: Ideology, Performance, Dialogue: Essays in Honor of John J. Peradotto.* Maryland: Rowman & Littlefield, 1999.

Poe, Joe Park. *Genre and Meaning in Sophocles'* Ajax. Frankfurt am Main, 1987.

Pucci, Pietro. *Oedipus and the Fabrication of the Father:* Oedipus Tyrannus *in Modern Criticism and Philosophy.* Maryland: Johns Hopkins University Press, 1992.

Rudnytsky, Peter L. *Freud and Oedipus.* New York: Columbia University Press, 1987.

——, and Ellen Handler Spitz, eds. *Freud and Forbidden Knowledge.* New York: New York University Press, 1994.

Schweizer, Harold. *History and Memory: Suffering and Art.* Pennsylvania: Bucknell University Press, 1998.

Scodel, Ruth. *Sophocles.* Boston: Twayne Publishers, 1984.

Scott, William C. *Musical Design in Sophoclean Theater.* Hanover: University Press of New England, 1996.

Segal, Charles. *Oedipus Tyrannus: Tragic Heroism and the Limits of Knowledge.* New York: Oxford University Press, 2001.

——. *Tragedy and Civilization: An Interpretation of Sophocles.* Norman: University of Oklahoma Press, 1999.

————. *Oedipus Tyrannus: Tragic Heroism and the Limits of Knowledge.* New York: Twayne Publishers, 1993.

Steiner, George. *Antigones.* Connecticut: Yale University Press, 1996.

Sullivan, Shirley Darcus. *Sophocles' Use of Psychological Terminology: Old and New.* Ottawa: Carleton University Press, 1999.

Travis, Roger. *Allegory and the Tragic Chorus in Sophocles'* Oedipus at Colonus. Maryland: Rowman & Littlefield Publishers, 1999.

Tymieniecka, Anna-Teresa. *Enjoyment: From Laughter to Delight in Philosophy, Literature, the Fine Arts and Aesthetics.* Boston: Kluwer Academic, 1997.

Tyrrell, William Blake. *Recapturing Sophocles'* Antigone. Maryland: Rowman & Littlefield Publishers, 1998.

Van Nortwick, Thomas. *Oedipus: the Meaning of a Masculine Life.* Norman: University of Oklahoma Press, 1998.

Vellacott, Philip. *An English Reader's Guide to Sophocles'* Oedipus Tyrannus *and* Oedipus Coloneus. England: Monophron, 1993.

Vernant, Jean-Pierre, and Pierre Vidal-Naquet, trans. Janet Lloyd. *Myth and Tragedy in Ancient Greece.* New York: Zone Books, 1990.

Waldock, A. J. A. *Sophocles the Dramatist.* Cambridge, U.K.: Cambridge University Press, 1966.

Whitman, Cedric Hubbell. *Sophocles; A Study of Heroic Humanism.* Cambridge: Harvard University Press, 1951.

Whitlock-Blundell, Mary. *Helping Friends and Harming Enemies: A Study in Sophocles and Greek Ethics.* Cambridge, U.K., and New York: Cambridge University Press, 1998.

Wilson, Joseph P. *The Hero and the City: An Interpretation of Sophocles'* Oedipus at Colonus. Ann Arbor: University of Michigan Press, 1997.

Winnington-Ingram, Reginald Pepys. *Sophocles: An Interpretation.* New York: Cambridge University Press, 1979.

Wohl, Victoria. *Intimate Commerce: Exchange, Gender, and Subjectivity in Greek Tragedy.* Austin: University of Texas Press, 1998.

Woodard, Thomas Marion, ed. *Sophocles: A Collection of Critical Essays.* Englewood Cliffs, New Jersey: Prentice-Hall, 1966.

Zak, William F. *The Polis and the Divine Order: The Oresteia, Sophocles, and the Defense of Democracy.* Pennsylvania: Bucknell University Press; London: Associated University Presses, 1995.

Zelenak, Michael X. *Gender and Politics in Greek Tragedy.* New York: Peter Lang, 1998.

Acknowledgments

The Language of Sophocles: Communality, Communication and Involvement by Felix Budelmann. © 2000 by Cambridge University Press. Reprinted by permission of Cambridge University Press.

Greek Tragedy: A Literary Study, 3rd ed. by H. D. F. Kitto. © 1961 by Methuen & Co., Ltd. Reprinted by permission of Thomson Publishing Services.

Lattimore, Richard. *The Poetry of Greek Tragedy,* pp. 82–84, © 1958 by Richard Lattimore. Reprinted by permission of The Johns Hopkins University Press.

Musurillo, Herbert. "Sunken Imagery in Sophocles' *Oedipus.*" *American Journal of Philology,* 1957, 38–40. © The Johns Hopkins University Press. Reprinted by permission of The Johns Hopkins University Press.

Tragedy: Shakespeare and the Greek Example by Adrian Poole. © 1987 by Basil Blackwell Ltd. Reprinted by permission of Blackwell Publishing.

Greek Tragic Theatre by Rush Rehm. © 1992 by Routledge, Inc. Reprinted by permission of Thomson Publishing Services.

Oedipus Tyrannus: *Tragic Heroism and the Limits of Knowledge* by Charles Segal. © 2001 by Oxford University Press. Reprinted by permission.

Collected Papers on Greek Tragedy by T. C. W. Stinton. © 1990 by Clarendon Press. Reprinted by permission of Oxford University Press.

Reprinted by permission of the publisher from "Irrational Evil" in *Sophocles: A Study of Heroic Humanism,* by Cedric H. Whitman. Cambridge, Mass.: Harvard University Press, Copyright © 1951 by the President and Fellows of Harvard College.

"Plain Words in Sophocles" by P. E. Easterling. From *Sophocles Revisited,* Jasper Griffin, ed. © 1999 by Oxford University Press. Reprinted by permission of Oxford University Press.

Theatrical Space and Historical Place in Sophocles' Oedipus at Colonus by Lowell Edmunds. © 1996 by Rowman & Littlefield Publishers, Inc. Reprinted by permission.

Index of
Themes and Ideas

AESCHYLUS, 9–11, 14, 15, 19, 36, 40, 41, 42, 43, 73, 93

ANTIGONE, 63, 71–95; Antigone contrasted with Creon in, 84–86; Antigone in, 71–72, 73, 74, 75, 76, 78, 79–80, 81, 82–83, 84–91, 92, 93, 94–95; Antigone's death in, 71–72, 75, 76; Antigone's opening address in, 82–83, 89–91, 95; burial of Polynices in, 71, 74, 75, 79–80, 82, 85, 86–87, 88–89, 90; characters in, 78; Chorus of Theban Elders in, 68, 72, 74–75, 76, 78, 84, 91, 94; Creon in, 71, 74, 75–76, 77, 78, 80, 81–82, 83–86, 87, 88, 90, 91, 93, 94, 95; critical views on, 79–95; Eteocles in, 74, 78, 88, 90; Eurydice in, 72, 76, 77, 78; Haemon in, 71–72, 75–77, 78; historical background of, 72–73; human and divine agency in, 93–95; invention in, 92–93; Ismene in, 71, 74, 75, 78, 84–86, 87, 89, 90–91, 95; literary origins of, 73–74, 81–83, 92–93; and *Oedipus at Colonus,* 64; plot summary of, 71–77; Polynices in, 71, 74, 76, 78, 79–80, 85, 86–87, 88–89, 90, 757; private conscience and public duty in, 71; psychological evolution of Antigone in, 88–89; recurring imagery in, 82–84; Tiresias in, 76, 78; watchmen in, 74, 75, 79–80, 86, 87

ARISTOPHANES, 93

ARISTOTLE, 14, 17, 38–39, 41, 81

CHORUS, 15, 16–17; in *Antigone,* 68, 72, 74–75, 76, 78, 84, 91, 94; in *Oedipus at Colonus,* 45, 46–48, 49–50, 51, 56–58, 67–68; in *Oedipus Rex,* 21–22, 24, 25, 26, 57, 68

DIONYSUS, 14, 15–16

ELECTRA, 66, 91; Aeschylus' *Libation-Bearers* compared with, 9–11

EURIPIDES, 14, 19, 36, 40, 41, 73, 92, 93

OEDIPUS AT COLONUS, 13, 45–70; and *Antigone,* 64; Antigone in, 45–46, 48, 49, 50, 51, 54, 55, 57, 58, 60, 63, 65; and authority of chorus, 67–68; characters in, 51; charging of themes through concentration and repetition in, 53, 54; Chorus of Elders of Colonus in, 45, 46–48, 49–50, 51, 56–58, 67–68; contradiction in, 53–54; Creon in, 45, 47, 48–49, 51, 64; critical views on, 52–70; Eteocles in, 45, 47, 51; historical background of, 45, 61–62; Ismene in, 45, 47, 48, 50, 53, 58, 60, 64; mythical background of, 45–46; and new image of civilization and outcast's reintegration into society, 64–66; Oedipus in, 43, 45–48,

49–50, 51, 53–54, 55–56, 57, 58–60, 61–62, 63–64, 65–66, 68, 69–70;
Oedipus' journey in, 58–60; Oedipus' moral innocence in, 43; and
Oedipus Rex, 62–64; oracle in, 45, 46, 47, 60, 62, 63–64; oscillation in,
53, 54; plot summary of, 45–50, 63; Polynices in, 45–46, 47, 49, 51, 66;
responsibility in, 69–70; staging of Oedipus' opening speech in, 55–56;
Theseus in, 46, 47, 48–49, 50, 51, 53, 66

OEDIPUS REX, 19–44, 63; Antigone in, 19, 20, 25, 26; audience of,
40–42; characters in, 26; Chorus of Old Men of Thebes in, 21–22, 24,
25, 26, 57, 68; Corinthian messenger in, 16, 24; Creon in, 16, 21,
22–23, 24, 25, 26, 29; critical views on, 27–44; as familiar Greek story,
29–30; and foundling story, 24, 31–32; Freud's interpretation of,
34–38; irony in, 19; Ismene in, 19, 20, 25, 26; Jocasta in, 20, 23–24, 26,
29, 37, 40, 43; Laius in, 19–20, 21, 23, 30, 31, 35, 37, 40, 41, 42, 43;
limits of Apollo's responsibility in, 27–29; and modern reader, 38–39;
mythical background of, 19–20, 21; and *Oedipus at Colonus*, 63–64;
Oedipus, King of Thebes in, 19, 20–25, 26, 27–29, 30, 31–32, 34–39,
40, 41, 42–44; and Oedipus' ill-fated quest for truth in, 23–24, 32, 35,
37, 39, 42–44; oracle in, 20, 21, 22, 23, 27–29, 30, 39, 40, 43, 63; plague
imagery in, 20–21, 32–34, 37, 39, 43, 44; plot structure of, 31–32; plot
summary of, 19–25; and riddle of Sphinx, 20, 22, 37, 38, 41, 43; and
standard version of Oedipus legend, 40–42; Tiresias in, 22, 23, 26, 29,
32, 38; and tragedy, 38–39

ORACLES, 17–18, 20; in *Oedipus at Colonus*, 45, 46, 47, 60, 62, 63–64; in
Oedipus Rex, 20, 21, 22, 23, 27–29, 30, 39, 40, 43, 63

PHILOCTETES, 36, 59, 65–66

SOPHOCLES: biography of, 12–13; and tragedy, 14, 15

TRAGEDY, 14–18; and *Oedipus Rex*, 38–39